Awel o'r Nef

Breeze from Heaven

Stories from Welsh Communities
1940s – 1980s

D. ERYL DAVIES

DayOne

© Day One Publications 2023

ISBN 978-1-84625-746-9

British Library Cataloguing in Publication Data available

Published by Day One Publications
Ryelands Road, Leominster, HR6 8NZ
Telephone 01568 613 740
North America Toll Free 888 329 6630
email—sales@dayone.co.uk
web site—www.dayone.co.uk

Cover design by smallprint

Printed by 4edge Limited

Contents

Foreword

The one great work that God is accomplishing in the world—the one thing that will stand for eternity—is the building of the Church of our Lord Jesus Christ. This happens when men and women are brought out of darkness and into light, those far off are drawn near, and those dead in trespasses and sins are given new, spiritual, eternal life.

God does this by the sovereign power of the Holy Spirit accompanying the proclamation of the gospel—God's good news in Jesus Christ.

This little book gives a number of vignettes of God's work in Wales between the 1940s and the 1980s. This was neither a period of revival nor of barrenness. It was a period when the gospel was recovered and safeguarded, local churches were strengthened and planted and people were saved. There was a longing among God's people for greater blessing, but in looking back, we are grateful for the blessing he gave us, and it is important that we learn its lessons. The sovereign God answered the prayers of his people and blessed their evangelism to the salvation of souls. As such, we are called to thankfulness and praise, to confidence in the gospel and in the power and goodness of God, to zealous evangelism and to earnest, believing prayer.

The number of examples given could be multiplied, and in reviewing the period, we will inevitably see weaknesses as well as strengths. But God has graciously blessed us. May these accounts stir us up to seek God for greater faithfulness and greater blessing in our own day.

Mark Thomas
General Secretary of the
Evangelical Movement of Wales

Preface

I was privileged to become a Christian in my late teens and afterwards had the additional privilege of serving the Lord as a minister of the gospel in Wales from the 1960s. Providentially, I have met some of the people mentioned in this book and also heard them preach. Converted in the aftermath of a powerful movement of the Holy Spirit in the 1940s and 1950s, when the Lord saved many young people in the university colleges in Wales, some of the men referred to occasionally recounted the Lord's dealings with them as they urged on us the need to know the Lord more intimately and to be passionate about the gospel. These men were devoted to prayer and encouraged us younger people to pray.

It has therefore been a pleasure researching this period in the history of a few gospel churches in mid-twentieth-century Wales, but the accounts of the Lord's work included in this book represent only a small sample of what the Lord did at that time in Wales. I am aware that other churches, including Pentecostal churches, also experienced blessing and growth during this period. I am grateful to all who have shared their memories with me and provided valuable primary sources. May our triune God, Father, Son and Holy Spirit, be praised.

D. Eryl Davies
January 2023

1. Introduction

Francis Schaeffer (1912–1984) was an American pastor, missionary and apologist who pioneered a valuable ministry in the L'Abri Fellowship in Switzerland from 1955. Young people from many countries began to visit L'Abri in great numbers for spiritual help and answers to their many questions. Schaeffer has been described as a man who 'lived in the present, learned from the past, and looked to the future'.[1] I love that description of the man, and that is how I view this book. As we consider what the Lord did in churches in mid-twentieth-century Wales, we must also face the realities of our present situation, while at the same time looking in faith to a period of greater progress in gospel work in the near future.

Here is a thrilling story and a reminder that the Lord can transform any church situation and save the most unlikely people.

Aims

This book has three aims: to inform, invite and inspire. The first aim is to inform readers of some of the ways the Lord blessed churches and preaching ministries to an unusual degree during the 1940s to the 1980s. Prayers were answered in encouraging and even unexpected ways. There have been occasional articles in local church magazines, but the story of these years is being told in book form for the first time. Many who witnessed and experienced these events have already died but some did share their memories which have been corroborated by those who knew them or were affected personally.

The second aim is to invite readers to think about the biblical principles and the passion governing the preaching and evangelism over this period in Wales. While the Lord is in control of all that happens in our lives, as well as

---

1 J. I. Packer, 'Francis Schaeffer: No Little Person' in *Collected Shorter Writings of J. I. Packer*. Vol. 4: *Honouring the People of God* (Carlisle, Cumbria: Paternoster Press, 1999) pp. 89–97.

in our churches and in the world, we still have responsibilities as Christians to pray and proclaim the gospel. In the work of the kingdom, the Lord uses his Word, blessed by the Holy Spirit, to bring people to faith and to edify believers. There are lessons to learn from the past and challenges to face if we are to experience more progress in evangelism and in local church preaching ministries.

The third aim is to inspire readers to pray and seek the Lord's powerful intervention once again in churches and in society. In reading the different accounts of the Lord's work, a strong emphasis on personal prayer and church prayer meetings is noticeable, as well as on clearly preaching the gospel of Christ to unbelievers in society, with the expectation of seeing conversions. The Lord certainly answered prayers! Can we be inspired and encouraged to pray for the Lord's help in evangelism and church life?

To illustrate the differences between the past and the present, in the next chapter attention is drawn to the sharp contrast between the 'then' and the 'now', a contrast that gripped me powerfully in the summer of 2017.

Questions

1. Consider ways in which you can, like Schaeffer, live in the present, learn from the past, yet look to the future in faith. Have you any suggestions to make?
2. How aware are you of the ways in which the Lord used gospel preaching so powerfully over the past eighty years?

2. Then and Now

In August 2017, my wife and I visited some revival sites in north-west Wales associated with the Beddgelert Revival of 1817–1821,[2] one of the most powerful regional revivals in the history of Wales. It was a thrill to be there again, but the visit was tinged with considerable sadness.

Capel-y-Nant

Located on the Lleyn Peninsula, Capel-y-Nant is the building of the Calvinistic Methodists or Presbyterian Church of Wales, which in 2017 had a large notice outside with the stark statement, 'For Sale'. The history of Capel-y-Nant is heart-warming. A small, thatched-roof house, Saethon Bach, had been used as a meeting-place for preaching and prayer from 1754. Gradually this building became too small for the numbers of people wanting to hear the preaching of the gospel, especially when revival broke out in 1780. So, in 1782, Capel-y-Nant was built less than one mile from Saethon Bach. Revival again broke out here in 1816 in answer to the prayers of believers and in subsequent years, too, there was considerable blessing. By 2017, however, there was no alternative but to place the attractive building on the market, as the membership of the church consisted of a mere handful of elderly people who were unable to attend services.

This is the reality of the 'now' situation in Wales. Many churches are reduced to a few aged members with little choice but to close and sell their buildings, which are often pulled down by developers or adapted as residential homes, garages, warehouses or clubs. This trend was being accelerated as a result of the COVID-19 lockdown.

---

2 Eryl Davies, *The Beddgelert Revival* (Bridgend: Bryntirion Press, 2004).

Hafod-y-Llan

We also visited the small farmhouse, Hafod-y-Llan, Gwynant, where Richard Williams, early in his preaching there one Sunday afternoon in August 1817, suddenly found himself unexpectedly preaching powerfully under the Holy Spirit's influence. The impact on flippant, worldly young people and adults was immediate and overwhelming. This farmhouse has now been renovated by the National Trust and rented out for holidays. However, we were able to stand with a small group of Christians in the room where Richard Williams once preached, to remember the time when revival broke out in that farmhouse precisely two hundred years previously and to pray together for the current situation. Although remembering the distant past—the 'then'—we recognised that, as interesting and moving as it was, it bore no resemblance to the 'now' situation in the area. We prayed about the desperate spiritual needs and asked the Lord to work powerfully once again in North Wales.

Bethania Church

Returning down the track from Hafod-y-Llan to the Capel Curig Road, we reached the junction, where, to our immediate right, stood Bethania Chapel. This building had been erected soon after the Beddgelert Revival for the large numbers of converts and 'hearers' who needed a more local church thus avoiding the long walk to the main Beddgelert chapel. Bethania had been the scene of much blessing, conversions and powerful preaching during its history, but the building had now become a community centre and tea room. Despite its exciting history, hardly anyone knew about its glorious past. Bethania was the 'then', but we were confronting the reality of the 'now'—a different situation and culture.

Sad

Possibly the saddest moment was in the village of Beddgelert itself, at the site where the large Calvinistic Methodist place of worship had once stood and in 1817 had experienced such an intense revival that it spread far and wide.

All that remained was a small piece of land surrounded by iron railings, with an inscription marking the location of the chapel. That church had exercised a strategic ministry in the past. To ensure that locals had the opportunity of hearing gospel preaching, the Beddgelert church had established a network of preaching stations throughout this extensive parish extending over an area of nine miles, including the farmhouse at Hafod-y-Llan. While the Lord's power came upon the preacher in Hafod-y-Llan during the summer of 1817, bringing many people under conviction of sin, it was some weeks later that the Lord visited the Beddgelert church in reviving power.

The spiritual and contemporary reality of the 'now' in the village of Beddgelert and in the surrounding area is dire. There is no other way to describe the situation. We were back in the 'now', far removed from the 'then' of the Beddgelert Revival of 1817–1821. What I have described relating to a few of the many revival sites in north-west Wales is true of other parts of the country and the United Kingdom as a whole. There is a warning for us here. We dare not be nostalgic, thinking only about past blessing or revivals, rather we must face seriously the reality and challenges of our contemporary situation. Prayer is needed—believing, persistent prayer for the Lord to intervene once again.

Tension

The tension between the past, present and future can be a difficult one to hold together in a balanced way. Our tendency is to swing from living nostalgically in the past to feeling discouraged in the present, while at the same time despairing of the future. Such imbalance is more common than is recognised and so we need to be challenged and that includes learning from what the Lord has done in the past among his people. It really is an exciting story and one we can benefit from in many ways.

In the next chapter we move closer to the story of blessing in churches from the 1940s to the 1980s by reminding ourselves of the context in which the Lord worked at that time. Although it was an extremely challenging and discouraging situation, we will eventually observe in subsequent chapters how prayer, gospel preaching and a passion to share the gospel with unbelievers were intertwined and inseparable. The Lord answered prayer. While they did not experience 'revival', yet there was a greater degree of blessing, resulting in many conversions and the enriching of churches and individual believers.

Questions

1. What is your response to the 'then' and 'now' contrast drawn in this chapter?
2. How do you understand revival and the work of the Holy Spirit? Notice:
   - What happened in Beddgelert in 1817–1821 is referred to as 'revival', which is shorthand for an 'extra-ordinary degree' of power given sovereignly by the Lord to the preaching of the gospel.
   - Revivals are for a limited period in which many people in a community are saved and believers in churches enlivened and given deeper experiences of the Lord.
   - The Holy Spirit is always at work in the church through the Word, in varying degrees of power. This is the ongoing work of the Holy Spirit in believers and in the preaching of the gospel.
   - From the 1940s to the 1980s, there was a greater degree of power and blessing on some preaching ministries, though it was not revival. This can happen at any time.
   - Christians are always indwelt by the Holy Spirit, who produces 'the fruit of the Spirit' (Galatians 5:22–23) in their lives. See also Romans 8:9.

3. Context

Here are a few dates and details to indicate the challenging context for what was happening in Wales during the period covered when many people were being converted.

1939–1945   75 million people in different countries died directly or indirectly as a result of the Second World War, including at least 20 million military personnel. Besides the loss of loved ones, many suffered physically, emotionally and psychologically. Hardships were experienced, including food rationing, compulsory employment for women and the evacuation of many children to rural areas from inner cities where there was heavy bombing.

1940–1950   Considerable blessing was experienced in university Christian Unions in Wales as students were converted and encouraged in their Christian lives.

1943   Dr D. Martyn Lloyd-Jones became the sole minister of Westminster Chapel, London, after being assistant minister there from 1938. He exercised a powerful and extensive preaching ministry until his retirement in 1968.

1944   An Education Act approved by Parliament required all schools to provide religious instruction and to begin each school day with corporate worship.

1945   John Stott began his ministry at All Souls Church, Langham Place, London, where over time his influence grew considerably. Many other evangelical ministries commenced in various key parts of Britain.

1945 Lloyd-Jones challenged radio listeners in Wales, 'Are we aware of this new situation?'[3] He stated that the religious climate was very different from even twenty years earlier; it was no longer a question of immorality 'but the total absence of morality'. Churches were less aware of these profound changes.

Post-war Social life drifted further away from Christian teaching and values as churches persisted in their critical interpretation of the gospel and denial of major Christian doctrines. More than anything, this hastened the numerical and spiritual decline. Churches were losing touch with the rising generation of children and young people and there was a desperate lack of faithful Bible teaching and gospel preaching.

1948–49 In North Wales especially, a powerful moving of the Holy Spirit upon students and young people resulted in many conversions and much blessing, as well as the launch of the Welsh language magazine *Y Cylchgrawn Efengylaidd*, intended for young people, believers and unbelievers.

1948 The National Health Service began under the leadership of Aneurin Bevan.

1948 The World Council of Churches was launched, creating tensions and divisions later for some evangelical churches over the following decades.

1949–1952 Revival broke out on the Isle of Lewis, Scotland.

1960–2000 An already declining church membership in Britain fell even further by 40 per cent, with the closure of 6,000 churches. At its peak in 1930, the ten million plus church members represented

---

3 Religion Today and Tomorrow, BBC Wales Radio 1945. D. M. Lloyd-Jones, *Knowing the Times: Addresses Delivered on Various Occasions 1942–1977* (Edinburgh: The Banner of Truth, 1989), pp. 14–31.

31 per cent of the adult population; by 2000, membership had fallen to 12 per cent and far lower by 2021.

Preparing the way for God's activity during the mid-decades of the twentieth century was the powerful preaching of Dr Martyn Lloyd-Jones in Sandfields Forward Movement Presbyterian Church, Aberavon, Port Talbot.[4] During the period 1927–1938 both the church and the locality were affected in an amazing way, resulting in the conversion of many people, including some notorious characters.[5] The number of converts and new church members increased significantly each year during this period. In 1931 as many as 128 people were converted 'from the world', with even more converts the following year. Undoubtedly there was a remarkable degree of the Holy Spirit's power on the preaching.

In south-west Wales, 1937 was a significant year when Idris Davies preached in Welsh language churches in the Llanpumpsaint, Cynnwyl, Llangeler and Carmarthen areas during the year. He worked as a junior school teacher and lived in Ammanford, but he was a gifted evangelist who gave himself to itinerant preaching whenever possible outside school hours. His preaching was powerful, resulting in a number of conversions, and the 'breeze of the Spirit' pervaded the services. It was early in these meetings that Glyn Owen was converted as a teenage reporter writing for the local newspaper. Other preachers too, like the Rev. Hywel Griffiths, Bridgend, were used powerfully in the area during this period.

---

4 The Presbyterian Church of Wales 'Forward Movement' was the name eventually given to the work of outreach to needy and unchurched industrial and urban areas of North and South Wales. Previously, it was known as the Church Extension and Mission Work Society. By 1907, forty-eight Forward Movement halls had been erected.

5 Born in 1899, Dr Martyn Lloyd-Jones was brought up in south-west Wales. The family moved to London when he was fourteen years old and at the age of sixteen he began to study medicine and had a brilliant medical career, becoming a Harley Street consultant physician briefly until he had an overwhelming 'call' from God to preach the gospel. After his time pastoring the South Wales church, he became the minister of Westminster Chapel, London. He was widely recognised as an outstanding preacher and many of his sermons, Bible studies and addresses have been published. He died in 1981. For a brief biography, read Eryl Davies, *Dr D. Martyn Lloyd-Jones* (Darlington: EP Books, 2011).

Reference could also be made to missionaries who left Wales to exercise influential ministries in other countries, even witnessing revival in the period from 1939 to the 1970s. That would demand another book and considerably more research. But to close this chapter, we record two examples of students holding missions in Welsh churches during the 1940s. They serve to illustrate how the Lord's work in the colleges benefited and encouraged churches in some areas of the country.

Llanelli 1945

A group of Christian university students had felt a deepening concern for their home town of Llanelli and, with other students, held an evangelistic mission there in the summer of 1945. This was not the first student-led mission to be held around this time in South Wales, but it was the most fruitful and had a major impact on local people and churches. The mission was held in Zion Baptist Church, the largest Free Church building in the town, with a seating capacity of over one thousand people. The student leaders preached each evening to packed congregations, except on the Wednesday evening when Arnold Aldis, a consultant surgeon in Cardiff, preached with considerable power. A number of people were converted that evening and during the mission many came to faith including about one hundred local young people. The open-air preaching by the students was also effective with hundreds of people listening, and was followed by serious conversations concerning the gospel. On the final evening it was even more remarkable as the students preached outside a cinema and in close proximity to a dance hall and hotel. Some of the traffic had to be diverted by police due to the congestion caused by the crowds gathering to hear the preaching.

Among the converts were young men who were later called into the Christian ministry, like John Thomas[6] and Hugh D. Morgan.[7] They were close friends and both sixth form pupils in Llanelli Grammar School. One

---

6   Born in 1927, he became pastor of Sandfields Presbyterian Church, Aberavon, Port Talbot, from 1953 until his unexpected death in April 1969. See also *Contender for the Faith: a tribute to J. B. E. Thomas, Bethlehem, Sandfields* (Bridgend: Evangelical Movement of Wales, 1975).

of the student leaders during this week remarked years later that the Llanelli 1945 mission was 'the most significant event of my life, my ministerial life, my life in evangelism ...'[8] That was no exaggeration, despite his illustrious Christian career.

The 1945 Llanelli mission is an example of how Christian students co-operated with local churches and received prayer support from local Christians before and after the mission. W. M. George was the pastor of Caersalem Welsh Baptist Church in Llanelli and he had been holding an inter-denominational monthly prayer meeting for Christians to seek the Lord's blessing on the town. On the chosen day each month, three prayer meetings were arranged—morning, afternoon and evening—so that those working shifts in local factories could attend at least one of the prayer times. There was a growing prayer concern for the town and one lady attending those prayer meetings had for years felt a burden for the Lord to bless students in the area.

Following a small student mission in Carmarthen in 1944, two students decided it would be right to meet for prayer during each college vacation, with the purpose of praying for Llanelli. When these two students, Gwyn Walters and Huw Davies, with other Llanelli students, felt constrained to hold this student-led mission in Llanelli in 1945, it was to the Rev. W. M. George and his monthly prayer group that they turned to for prayer support, but they also met regularly during the vacations in the homes of local Christians.

Bala 1948

Instances of the unusual degree of the Lord's blessing on student evangelism in this period are numerous, but our second example takes us to the small, historic town of Bala in Gwynedd, North Wales, where a mission was held

---

7   He became the pastor of Bethany Presbyterian Church, Gelli, and Duffryn, in the Rhondda Valley 1953–1962, then Malpas Road Presbyterian Church, Newport from 1962 until he died suddenly in 1992. The church seceded from the denomination in 1976 and became Malpas Road Evangelical Church.

8   Geraint D. Fielder, *'Excuse Me, Mr Davies—Hallelujah!': Evangelical Student Witness in Wales 1923–1983* (Bridgend/Leicester: Evangelical Press of Wales/Inter-Varsity Press, 1983), p. 119.

by students. Once again, as in Llanelli, there was a remarkable degree of blessing, but the background is important. A significant number of students had been converted in Welsh University Colleges, including Bangor, between 1948 and 1952. In 1947, Elwyn Davies, a Bangor student, experienced forgiveness of sin. A retreat in Dolgellau in January 1948 was signally blessed when numbers of young people were converted. Later in the same month, the Bangor students held their own retreat in Betws Garmon, where several came to trust the Lord for salvation. The Bangor Christian Union later agreed with young people in Bala to hold a mission in their town over Easter 1948 under the leadership of the Rev. I. D. E. Thomas, a young Welsh Baptist pastor in Glanaman, South Wales. Elwyn Davies and Arthur Pritchard, a Welsh Presbyterian minister in north-west Wales, agreed to assist him in leading the mission.

Driving into Bala before the mission started, Elwyn Davies and Arthur Pritchard felt desperately nervous especially when they passed the Presbyterian College. On the third evening of the preaching meetings, blessing broke out with numbers of people coming to saving faith in Christ and so the meetings were extended for an additional week. A few of the older Christians who remembered the 1904 revival in the town remarked that some of the preaching meetings and the Lord's felt presence were similar to what was experienced in that revival.

Questions

1. What strikes you as being important on reading about the student missions in Llanelli and Bala?
2. How significant was prayer, especially in the Llanelli mission? What lessons can we learn from that example?

4. Some Effective Ministries in the 1940s

Idris B. Davies

Converted in the south-west of England, Rev. I. B. Davies, affectionately referred to as 'IB', returned to South Wales where both he and his wife became members of the Presbyterian Church in Sandfields, Aberavon. Lloyd-Jones, who was the pastor at the time, recognised that IB was called to the ministry, but only after he had accepted the challenge to learn New Testament Greek. IB's theological and pastoral training in the denominational college was completed by the summer of 1940. He had two churches in Pontypridd for his first pastorate from 1940 to 1945—Hermon, Maesycoed, and Park, Treforest.

The Rev. Andrew Davies, the younger son of IB, has no personal memories of this period in his father's ministry being too young at the time, 'But', he writes, 'I have heard from my parents and others of some of the things that happened.' He continues:

> As in many Welsh chapels there were church members and adherents who were unconverted. They needed to be convicted, brought to true repentance and given saving faith in Christ. My father's preaching was direct, bold and evangelistic. Remarkable conversions occurred under his preaching although we have no indication of the number. On one occasion after a cremation at Glyntaff Crematorium, the officer in charge showed my father what happened when the coffin and body of the deceased were incinerated. It had a profound effect on him. Shortly afterwards he preached what has been described as the cremation sermon in which he spoke powerfully and urgently about the reality of hell and the glory of the death and resurrection of Christ as the only way of escape. Many were deeply affected and converted, including a young man, Alan Rees (later to become a

science professor at a Canadian university) whose mother had recently died. Following the sermon, Alan spent the Sunday night at his mother's grave, seeking the Lord for mercy. At the crack of dawn on Monday morning he knocked at the door of the manse to tell my parents that the Lord had come to him and saved him.

Bessy Jones

Another conversion was that of 'Aunty Bessy' Jones. She was a character who thought early on that she could love the world and profess to be a Christian at the same time. But she was told by IB in no uncertain terms that she would dance her way to hell. She was broken and transformed by the grace of God and became a wonderful encourager of young men preparing for the ministry and a great example of ardent, practical love for Christ. For a few years, Aunty Bessy was later a matron and cook for campers in the Evangelical Movement of Wales (EMW) centre in Bryn-y-groes, Bala, where she was greatly loved and exercised an important spiritual ministry amongst campers and officers. On a visit to Westminster Chapel, London, she told Dr Martyn Lloyd-Jones that he was her spiritual grandfather because she believed (mistakenly)[9] that I. B. Davies had been converted under the Doctor's ministry in the 1930s in Sandfields and that she had been converted under IB. The Doctor was not amused! Many other people were converted and added to these two churches during IB's ministry.

Saltmead Hall 1945–1950

This place was established in 1895 as a mission hall under the Forward Movement of the Presbyterian Church of Wales in the tough, red-light district of Grangetown in the south-west area of Cardiff. It was then incorporated into the Glamorgan Presbytery East in 1898 with the church building officially opened in 1902.

---

9 IB had been converted in Somerset before attending Sandfields Church where Dr Lloyd-Jones was the pastor.

Many people were converted at Saltmead Hall during the following decades and in 1945 a strong evangelistic ministry was urgently needed. It was IB who rose to this huge challenge. Andrew Davies writes:

> *Under the preaching of my father many were converted, some from the nominal attendees and some from the area. As a result, quite a number entered the pastoral ministry, including my brother, Wynford, who also played rugby for Wales in the Victory Internationals following the end of the Second World War. Although I was too young to understand and appreciate all that was said from the pulpit, I was very conscious of the presence of God in the meetings and it has since made me realise the importance of the Spirit in the congregation as well as with the preacher. 'With You is the fountain of life; in Your light we see light.' When God is present, light shines around us and in us. One of the features of the ministry during my father's time in Saltmead was the gathering of young people for special times of mission and outreach. This not only brought young people together in fellowship but also helped them engage in prayerful, ongoing evangelism and church planting.*[10]

Open-air preaching

IB engaged regularly in open-air preaching during his ministry in Cardiff, then later in Neath. It is no surprise that he was invited by his local Glamorgan East Presbytery to address its ministers and church elders on the subject. The title of his discourse was 'The Church in the Open-Air'. He underlined the fact that 'so much of our Lord's work was done in the open air … the open air was his forum', though he acknowledged that the climate in Wales was very different from that of the Holy Land. 'The apostles, to a considerable degree, followed the Master's method', as did Wesley, Whitefield and the Calvinistic Methodist preachers in Wales in the eighteenth-century. IB continued:

---

10 Email correspondence, 20 November 2015.

So far as statistics inform us, it seems that today only about one in ten of our population is in church and it is patent to all that our ordinary methods do not get the people in. Therefore, there is a case for open-air preaching and testifying.

He insisted that, whether laymen or ministers, those preaching in the open-air

should prepare themselves as carefully, though differently, for work in the open-air as for work in the pulpit. Some amongst us think that our colleges could do something, or more, to prepare students for this work, for ... there is surely a right and a wrong technique! The message then should be straight and in language understandable by the people. It should never be apologetic, but should tell men and women that, without God, they do not live in any vital sense, and that by His grace there are possibilities for them that they have not guessed at. If there is to be singing, let it be the best; invite a choir and young people to support the minister. Let Elders, too, take their turn, and all be done decently and in order ... To my friends, ministerial and others, in Presbytery, I would say 'Is not open-air work at least worth our serious consideration?'

For IB, open-air preaching was a useful and important way of reaching the many unchurched people with the good news of the gospel. He was committed to taking advantage of this open door, whenever possible and he did so with great effect. We will refer later to his powerful ministry in Neath from 1950 to 1962.

Billy Graham

A significant visitor to South Wales in 1946 was the then unknown American evangelist, Billy Graham (1918–2018). Youth for Christ International appointed him in 1945 as their first full-time evangelist but it was not until his influential tent campaign in Los Angeles in 1949 that Graham began to be recognised internationally as a gifted evangelist. Graham's initial trip to the

UK was in March and April 1946 when, with five others in the team, he spent several nights at Hildenborough Hall in Kent, where the evangelist Tom Rees was based and where he was able to meet some key UK Christian leaders. At the time, Stephen Olford, a youth evangelist from Newport, South Wales, was the closing speaker in a youth conference being held there. His address on Ephesians 5:18, 'be filled with the Spirit', made a powerful impression on Graham who felt the need to know the Lord better. Graham explained, 'I was seeking for more of God in my life and I felt that here was a man who could help me.'

Gorseinon

On his second visit to the UK, Graham met with Olford. Speaking in Bristol first, Graham and his team then made their way to South Wales, arriving in Gorseinon in mid-October 1946. Graham preached in Caersalem Free Church, Gorseinon, on Monday 14 October but, because of the crowds wanting to hear the evangelist, the meeting was moved for the Tuesday evening to Zion Baptist Church, which had a much larger seating capacity.

David Ebenezer, converted in the 1904–05 revival, led Caersalem Church at the time but he was also President of Youth for Christ in Wales and had a passion for evangelism. Ebenezer had arranged for the National Young Life Campaign evangelist David Shepherd to speak in a series of evangelistic meetings in Caersalem. When Graham's availability was known, he was invited to preach at the two final meetings of that outreach. The impact of the preaching was considerable, with numbers of people saved, including Geraint Fielder who describes the evening he became a Christian:

> At that time, I was eleven and had started my second year in Grammar School. My first recollection of the events was Cliff Barrows, the sunny song leader, going down the High Street to Zion Chapel, playing to a trombone and crowds of people building up. I had a seat with my father in the front centre of the gallery. We must

have gone quite early. There was a huge congregation, some sitting on benches down both aisles, even up the pulpit steps.[11]

Fielder then describes the preaching:

Billy preached on 'you are weighed in the balances (scales) and found wanting', a text from the dramatic account of Belshazzar's feast (Daniel 5). I was convicted by the picture he drew of the contrast between God's perfection on one side of the scales and how my sinful life would never satisfy his standard — the scales were weighed against me. The preacher's presentation of Christ as the substitute for sinners who stepped in on the sinner's side to even out the scales I saw as my only hope.

Graham adopted a form of response which was unfamiliar to reformed churches in Wales, but a measure which had gained ground in the period. Fielder explains:

There was a fairly long appeal at the end and many people, perhaps dozens, went down and were led into a back room. Sitting where I was, I had a good view of all this and I was battling inside and felt I ought to have gone to the front but sat rooted. Eventually my dad turned to me and asked if I wanted to go down.

Fielder went down to the front, but it was difficult finding his way past the benches and when he reached the vestry door it was closed. To his relief, Billy Graham opened the door and spoke with him. Fielder was serious and 'meant business' in responding to the gospel that evening and for many years he went on to serve the Lord in student ministry and in church pastorates.

Whatever view one takes of such appeals following a gospel message, many that evening, like Geraint Fielder, were genuinely converted.

---

11 www.welldigger.blogspot.com/2012/03/billy-graham-encounters-holy-spirit.in.html. Confirmed in *'Excuse me, Mr Davies—Hallelujah!'* by Geraint Fielder, p. 101.

Pontypridd

Billy Graham and his team then moved to the Pontypridd area and this is where he met up again with Stephen Olford and they spent the best part of two days in prayer and studying the Word. The first evening, Graham spoke to a small congregation at Penuel, and Olford described his preaching as 'ordinary'. The next day Olford shared with Graham some of his own experience of the Lord and emphasised the need for brokenness. Later, as the two men prayed, Olford reported that

> *all heaven broke loose in that dreary little room. It was like Jacob laying hold of God and crying, 'Lord, I will not let Thee go except Thou bless me.'*

That evening, as Graham preached in a large Welsh Baptist church his preaching was transformed. He again preached from Daniel chapter 5 on Belshazzar's feast and there was a sense of awe upon the congregation. The response at the end was almost chaotic as many in the congregation surged to the front 'kneeling and broken'. Emotionalism? Were people moved by the music or the accent and eloquence of the American evangelist? Some were undoubtedly affected in that way, but there were many who genuinely trusted in Christ and began to walk with the Lord from that evening. The *Pontypridd Observer* carried news of the meeting the following week.

In his autobiography,[12] Graham does not provide detail of his time in Wales, except to refer to the food rationing and the poor quality of food given him!

Emrys Davies

The Rev. Richard Emrys Davies became the pastor of Mount Pleasant Baptist Church, Swansea, in 1947 and remained there until 1961. Under his ministry, the church soon became one of the most thriving evangelical Baptist churches in Wales. Married with two children, Bethan and Emyr,

---

12 *Just As I Am: The Autobiography of Billy Graham* (San Francisco: Harper, Zondervan, 1997).

he was a dynamic preacher, evangelist and noted singer. His first pastorate had been in Caersalem, Swansea, from 1936 to 1947, then, after pastoring Mount Pleasant, he became the pastor of Rye Lane Chapel, Peckham, from 1961 to 1975. Despite the impact of his ministry in Mount Pleasant, there are few available extant sources describing the man and his ministry, but a clear picture does emerge of his influential ministry even from the limited data available to the author.

Evangelism

Davies was essentially an evangelist. He had a powerful voice for preaching and often broke into singing a gospel song in English or Welsh during his Christ-centred preaching. Celebrating his fifth anniversary as pastor, the church magazine editor wrote:

> ... the services of the day were richly blessed. The messages were straight and forceful, inspired of God. These are days in which there is no time for 'milky sops'; we need 'strong meat' to withstand the onslaughts of the devil. The large congregations every Sunday testify to the power of his preaching.

That same summer Davies had received an invitation from "the Rev. Dr Oswald Smith to conduct a series of meetings at 'The Peoples Church', Toronto, and also to visit a number of Evangelical centres in the States". This would have involved him preaching 'at some of the leading churches of Canada and America'. While recognising the honour being extended to him and the church through this invitation, Davies

> declined the invitation because he felt that it was not the opportune time for him to be away from our church for a period of two months or more. To have made this decision must have meant much sacrifice for both Mr and Mrs Davies, and it further reveals their unstinted devotion to the work of the Kingdom at Mount Pleasant.

The church's desire was that 'God will permit him to remain with us for many years.'[13]

In 1954 the local newspaper reported that 'a queue formed outside Mount Pleasant an hour before the harvest festival service was due to start'. A public address system was used to relay the service to people outside and 'some had to be turned away but the pastor relieved the situation by getting some regular worshippers to give up their seats for those who did not usually attend church.' Davies' powerful gospel preaching resulted both in large congregations and in many professions of faith in the Lord Jesus Christ. His gospel sermons were always accompanied by an appeal for people to come forward and accept Christ.

Campaigns

In addition to his own preaching in Mount Pleasant, Davies encouraged the church to hold regular evangelistic campaigns, with visiting preachers from the UK and America. Two campaigns in April and July 1951 were sponsored by the Young People's Fellowship, who reported that they

felt it laid upon our hearts to pray for the manifestation of God's power and after much prayer and supplication, we can report well of these manifold blessings which have come and still are coming our way.

While the young people's second campaign in July was not so well attended, 'the services were a source of spiritual refreshment'. The April outreach was more encouraging. The campaign organised by the church was scheduled for 21–31 May 1951 under the title of 'The Faith of Our Fathers' and conducted by Dr Hyman J. Appleman and Rev. Jack Rollings. *The Messenger* reports:

For a year and more, prayers have been offered for an outpouring of the Holy Spirit and there is no doubt that the visit of Dr Appleman and the Rev. Jack Rollings was an answer to

---

13 *Messenger*, p. 5.

prayer. Scenes have been witnessed which were reminiscent of the Welsh Revival. Prayer meetings were started at 7.30 am and attended by more than 100 people, when the Presence of the Holy Spirit was manifest. All ages shared in the experiences and felt richly blessed and inspired. The whole town felt the immediate impact, the church was filled on every occasion and the services had to be relayed to the schoolroom. Loudspeakers were outside the church … Young and old people shared in outdoor work, distributing tracts and inviting all and sundry to come and share in the meetings.

On average about 2,000 people attended the meetings, with Christians often giving up their seats for visitors. They then went to another part of the building to hold a prayer meeting. Groups from other churches hired special coaches to attend the meetings, with the Mayor of Swansea giving his verbal support.

Without giving approval to the 'appeal' system or accepting that all professions of faith were genuine, it is clear that the campaign bore spiritual fruit. Acknowledging that 'the real results are known only to God', the church reported the following statistics from the campaign:

Adult decisions	272
Linked to other churches	110
Ready for baptism	43
Restorations	9
To be visited	101
Children's decisions	217

After examination and preparation, twenty-four people were baptised, forty-one people received into church membership in the communion service on 1 July and on 15 July another fifteen baptised. Many people were genuinely saved and continued to live for the Lord.

Welsh magazine

Few people know that Emrys Davies was one of three pastors who comprised the Editorial Board of the new Welsh language evangelical magazine, Y *Cylchgrawn Efengylaidd*, which was launched in November/December 1948. The other two members were the Revs. I. D. E. Thomas of Glanaman, and J. D. Williams, who was the Welsh Presbyterian minister in Bethany, Ammanford. It is no surprise that Davies was involved with this magazine for he was fluent in the Welsh language, but he would also have been thrilled hearing of the remarkable work of God taking place amongst students in the colleges in Wales, especially in the North. The magazine itself arose out of those Bala preaching meetings in 1948. The young people in the town requested that a magazine should be available to them for their own spiritual growth and which they could also give to unbelieving friends. They wanted the magazine to be simple, readable and challenging, yet faithful to the Bible.

What evangelicals believe

The opening article in the first issue of the magazine was by Lloyd-Jones, where he explained what evangelicals believe, approaching the subject within a biblical, historical context. He identified three emphases, the first being that of authority. For evangelicals, it is the Bible, rather than reason or feelings or a church, which determines what they believe and practise. The second emphasis is that of the gospel, with its unique message of salvation from sin through the substitutionary death of Jesus Christ on the cross for sinners. The third emphasis is that of the life of the Christian, beginning with the miracle of the new birth, then continuing with the indwelling, sanctifying work of the Holy Spirit in all believers.

What kind of faith?

Emrys Davies wrote the second article, which was evangelistic and contemporary—'What kind of faith do you have?' This 'is one of the most important questions', based on words in Acts 3:16, which he applied in three ways. First, genuine saving faith is a challenge to unbelievers. Second, saving faith exposes the failure of a lifeless religion and, thirdly, saving faith glorifies the triune God as people believe and depend on him while seeking to honour him. Davies ended the article by pleading with his readers: 'It is a time to praise God for His grace and love. Lift high the name of Jesus and glory in His cross.'[14] This was typical of Emrys Davies, the evangelist who delighted in proclaiming the gospel of Christ and honouring Jesus Christ as the only Saviour of sinners.

There is no record of him writing any additional articles, possibly due to the pressures of his own ministry, but also to the encouragement given to gifted younger men who were emerging in Wales to be involved as contributors. Nevertheless, Davies remained on the editorial board for nearly six years.

Retirement

Following his retirement from the ministry in London in 1975, Davies and his wife moved to live in the Cardigan area of west Wales. In the later months of his life, as a consequence of suffering from diabetes, both his legs were amputated but his faith remained radiant and the gospel never lost its thrill. The Revs. John Davies and Luther Rees, both serving in pastorates in the Swansea area at that time, visited him. John Davies[15] recalls his triumphant faith and peace in anticipating being with the Lord Jesus whom he loved with all his heart. Emrys Davies died on 14 May 1980 and his funeral service was held in Cardigan a week later. 'A Triumphant Service of Thanksgiving' was arranged in Mount Pleasant Church for 18 June under the chairmanship of the Rev. A. Glyn Morris. The closing message was delivered by a close friend, the Rev. Paul Tucker.

---

14 *Y Cylchgrawn Efengylaidd*, Vol. 1, No. 1, November/December 1948, pp. 9–16.
15 Email correspondence 10 January 2018: Rev. John Davies (1938–2019).

Questions

1. What are your main impressions after reading this chapter?
2. Young people under I. B. Davies' ministry in Saltmead, Cardiff, met for fellowship, prayer and evangelism. What place does prayer and evangelism have in our lives today?
3. Are there any details in the stories of Billy Graham and Emrys Davies which challenge you?

5. Effective Ministries in the 1950s

Here are some useful facts and dates pertaining to the 1950s which help to set the scene.

1950s   In Britain, many of the five million teenagers with their distinctive culture and an estimated £800 million to spend enjoyed rock 'n roll.

1950   North Korea invaded South Korea; for three years the Korean War took its toll with troops from Britain, America and Allies under the United Nations helping the beleaguered South Korean army.

1952   King George VI died and Princess Elizabeth became Queen.

1953   The Cold War between East and West reached its peak. Stalin died.

1954   Billy Graham held his evangelistic campaign in Haringey Arena, London.

1955   The Banner of Truth Magazine was launched.
ITV, a commercial TV station, was opened to begin a new era of television in Britain.

1956   James I. Packer's influential *Fundamentalism and the Word of God* was published, upholding the veracity of Scripture and encouraging confidence amongst Christians in God's infallible Word. This was a valuable resource for many Christians and pastors.

1957   Prime Minister Harold Macmillan reported that 'most of our people have never had it so good'. Austerity was replaced by an abundance of goods and freedom of choice. The Banner of Truth Trust was formed.

1958   John Stott's book *Basic Christianity* was published. The book contained evangelistic addresses delivered in university missions across Britain. The book was widely used and also translated into many languages. Sermons preached by Lloyd-Jones in Westminster Chapel, London, in the 1950s began to be published; the books continue to help Christians worldwide.

Gwyn Walters[16]

Memorial Hall in Cardiff is another of the many Forward Movement churches established under the Presbyterian Church of Wales, but its gospel ministry had become blurred after the Second World War and by 1950 the spiritual condition of the church was mixed and compromised. Rev. Dr Gwyn Walters' six years of ministry in Memorial Hall commenced in 1950 and was, in fact, his only pastorate in Wales. Keith David[17] was about eleven years of age when he heard that a new pastor was coming. He remembers it previously as a social church; he himself was in the Band of Hope, the Life Boys, otherwise known as the Junior Boys Brigade. Keith was also in the children's choir and recalls that a highlight of the Tuesday evening choir practices 'was the weekly raffle while every year there was the … pantomime which was always Coughdrop and the Seven Twerps'.

Keith attended the local junior school and Cardiff High School, where he befriended Brian Norton.[18] Brian attended the Boys Brigade on invitation from Keith, which in turn led him into the church just before Gwyn Walters arrived as pastor. At the age of thirteen, Brian came to personal faith in the Lord Jesus Christ under the powerful preaching of Walters.[19] Still in his teens, Brian also attended a series of lectures by Walters on the theology of grace, that were delivered in Cardiff under the auspices of London Bible College.

'Dramatic turn round'

Keith David explains that there was 'much religious activity' in the church, but he cannot recall hearing the gospel preached clearly until 1950. Church members looked forward to the arrival of a new minister and many said it

---

16 Gwyn Walters (1922–1993) left Cardiff in 1956 for the United States to teach theology; by 1962 he was Professor of Homiletics at the Gordon-Conwell Theological Seminary in Massachusetts.

17 Letter kindly provided by Keith David, with his memories of Memorial Hall, 4 March 2019.

18 Brian Norton (1939–2015) studied in London, attended Westminster Chapel for three years and was a science teacher for several years before becoming a Presbyterian minister in Durham. For his obituary, see *Evangelical Times*, September 2015.

19 Information provided by Brian's widow, Brenda Norton, who herself attended Memorial Hall as a believer halfway through Gwyn Walters' ministry. Email: 08/03/2019.

'would be good for the young people'. They were right, but not in the way they expected for Dr Walters 'brought with him a ministry that was quite new to the congregation'. The result was 'that about half the congregation left and the other half were converted!' Brenda Norton confirms that 'there was a dramatic turn round in the six years Gwyn Walters was there. Numbers of people left, and others came in.' The children's choir folded and the Boys Brigade moved to another church and, Keith explains, 'I was hearing a new vocabulary. People were using terms such as "saved" and "born again" which I had never heard in the chapel before'. Brenda Norton agrees that

> *there were numerous conversions during those six years and I would guess a reviving of a number of long-term members who hadn't had much solid teaching for a long time. A number of young people came to faith who keep the faith to this day.*

Brenda refers to the personal benefits of Walters' preaching ministry 'which was very considerable for me in laying a solid foundation, as well as for Brian'. Keith David explains, 'there were so many new enthusiastic converts. They wanted to be of service.' One of these converts was Keith's Sunday School teacher, who regularly gave his testimony to the class, 'telling us how wonderful it was to be a Christian … he certainly prayed for us even though he did not teach us much'.

'Remarkable event'

One incident during this period of ministry deserves mention. Keith David refers to the 'remarkable event' one Whit Sunday when the Sunday School Anniversary was being held. The Sunday evening congregation was much larger than usual as parents had come to watch their children taking part in the service. The weather was extremely hot and all the church doors were wide open. Gwyn Walters changed his prepared message and instead preached on the personal return of the Lord in glory. He was explaining the suddenness and unexpectedness of the event, but clearly struggled to find words adequate to emphasise the point. As he repeated the words 'it's going to come like ...', suddenly one of the church doors slammed shut with a loud crash. Everybody jumped. There had been no wind or human intervention and the preacher said that God had shut that door! The people had heard a powerful message.

Brenda Norton reminds us of the weekly prayer meetings:

> *I'm sure Brian would mention the weekly prayer meeting. The core group of young people would be regularly there. You wouldn't want to miss it. And they would regularly take part in prayer too. People would pray ... often very earnestly, and on occasions with tears.*

When Walters moved to America, Dr Eifion Evans became pastor and was followed by the Revs. A. L. Hughes and then Aerwyn (Mark) Pearce. 'During their ministries the church carried on in its re-discovered evangelical position' writes Keith David. Later, Keith had the joy of seeing both his mother and father converted under the faithful, biblical ministry of Pearce.

J. Elwyn Davies

Rev. J. Elwyn Davies (1925–2007) received his academic training for the Christian ministry in Bangor but, due to his burden for evangelism and the need to counsel growing numbers of people desiring spiritual help, he withdrew from his postgraduate BD course in favour of a less pressurised course of theological studies. He accepted an invitation to pastor Jerusalem Welsh Congregational Church in Blaenau Ffestiniog, North Wales, and was inducted to the pastorate in September 1950. During his five-year ministry, Elwyn's 'influence on the church and the locality was substantial',[20] although detailed information is lacking. The church had been established in 1869 and Elwyn was fearful of taking pastoral charge of a church with so many members. He need not have worried for he was warmly welcomed and supported. He appreciated the respect for God shown by members and

---

20 John Emyr, ed., *A Father in the Faith: J. Elwyn Davies, 1925–2007* (Bridgend: Bryntirion Press, 2012), p. 47. The Welsh version is *Porth yr Aur: Cofio J. Elwyn Davies*, golygwyd gan John Emyr (Pen-y-bont ar Ogwr: Gwasg Bryntirion, 2011), p. 49.

church officers. One example was the church secretary, who regularly pleaded in prayer 'for the express protection of heaven, arguing that Jerusalem was like a city set upon a hill that could not be hid'. Another officer confessed with tears in prayer often:

> Ni allaf roddi fel y rhoddaist im;
> I cannot give as thou hast given me;
> 'Rwy'n gweld, yng ngolau'r groes, fy ngorau'n ddim.
> My best is nothing, seen at Calvary.

The Holy Spirit blessed the preaching of the Word and Elwyn remembers with gratitude the discussions and the fervent prayers in the young people's prayer meeting on a Sunday afternoon and in the mid-week meetings.

> *The small vestry was often fairly full for a seiat or prayer meeting … Some of the children of the church began to meet together of their own accord on Friday evenings. There was given to them a missionary zeal greater than was to be seen in any other aspect of the church … They met together, they pastored each other. Before every meeting … they held their own prayer meeting with the majority of them taking part.*

'Breeze from heaven'

What was the explanation of this response on the part of children and young people in the church? Elwyn was in no doubt as to the answer:

> *It came from heaven, ever the source of quickening life … its fruit remains today … it was no flash in the pan, nor yet the fruit of natural effort. A breeze from heaven passed by and, as one who had the privilege of being present, I now know what I believed then, that in the pure, unpolluted breath of those same divine breezes lies the hope of the continuation of the gospel's witness in our land.*[21]

---

21 *A Father in the Faith*, pp. 130–131; *Porth yr Aur*, pp. 124–125.

Church membership

For the young people and others seeking membership in Jerusalem Church, Elwyn taught the Bible faithfully and questioned them concerning their faith, stressing the importance of trusting in the Lord Jesus Christ before formally entering church membership. The Lord dealt savingly with many of them in this way and they shared their experience with friends in school. Because so many young people were involved in becoming Christians or were interested in knowing more about the gospel, it was arranged for a Scripture Union meeting to be held in the church vestry. Numbers of the young people went to the home of Elwyn and Mair Davies seeking spiritual direction and counselling. Herbert Evans assisted Elwyn in caring for these young converts and continued to do so after Elwyn left. There was certainly 'a breeze' from heaven felt amongst these young people.

Other areas

This work of grace in the lives of young people, as well as adults, was repeated in other areas in the North like Llangollen, Dyffryn Nantlle, Botwnnog and Bangor.[22] In 1952, for example, several pupils in a Llangollen school trusted in the Lord Jesus, and one result of this was the introduction of lunch-time meetings and then, later, an after-school meeting on Thursdays. Fellowship and the study of the Bible were important to them. Other groups also emerged in Pwllheli, Porthmadog and Caernarfon and Herbert Evans organised rallies for these young people to provide them with fellowship, encouragement and teaching.

The young people assisted the older Christians in several ways. For example, they held open-air meetings, distributed Christian leaflets, gave away free copies of *Challenge*, a Christian newspaper, in places like Llandudno, and also held services in the local hospital. They expressed concern for those in need in Europe by sending out parcels of good quality clothes for the poor. On other occasions,

---

22 Noel Gibbard, *Cofio Hanner Canrif: Hanes Mudiad Efengylaidd Cymru 1948–1998* (Pen-y-bont ar Ogwr: Gwasg Bryntirion, 2000), pp. 43–45; *The First Fifty Years: The History of the Evangelical Movement of Wales 1948–98*, Noel Gibbard (Bridgend, Bryntirion Press, 2002), pp. 40–43.

they relaxed on a Saturday by meeting together for a picnic or a walk. These young Christians were respected by many people, but there was opposition too. When one young Christian wrote an essay on 'Conversion', the teacher became angry, but then discovered that many in his class had also become Christians. The Lord had done an extensive work of grace amongst the young people.

Scattered believers

Towards the end of his ministry in Jerusalem Church, one afternoon Elwyn and a close colleague, Arthur Pritchard, who pastored a Presbyterian Church some miles away, met to assess what was developing spiritually, especially in North Wales. They walked on a mountain near Blaenau Ffestiniog, both feeling a concern for the small scattered groups of believers emerging in various parts of North Wales. Elwyn was burdened and said, 'Someone has got to give his ministry to care for this work that is emerging.'[23]

'Dovetailing of providence'

Almost at the same time as Elwyn and Arthur met to express concern for the work in North Wales, Dr Douglas Johnson and Dr Lloyd-Jones in London were discussing the student work in Wales. They also shared the need for a successor to the Rev. Gwilym Roberts who had been pastoring the Christian Unions in Welsh University Colleges. Gwilym had accepted a call to minister at a Presbyterian Church in Tredegar, South Wales. On Lloyd-Jones's recommendation, Dr Johnson, who was General Secretary of the Inter-Varsity Fellowship to which the Christian Unions were affiliated, approached Elwyn at a time when the Evangelical Movement of Wales also needed Elwyn to care for fellowships of believers in Wales and develop the work, so there was 'the dovetailing of providence'. In 1955, Elwyn left Jerusalem Church in Blaenau Ffestiniog convinced that it was God's will to accept the invitation to care for university Christian Unions while at the same time developing the work of the EMW throughout Wales.

---

23 *'Excuse me, Mr Davies—Hallelujah!'*, p. 148.

Holywell

Holywell is a small town in north-east Wales on the Dee estuary, almost midway between Chester and Rhyl. The English Presbyterian Church in the town had an evangelical pastor, Gwyddno Rowlands, who had been a missionary with the Presbyterian Church of Wales in India for a brief period. He was succeeded in 1958 by the Rev. Gwilym Roberts. A spiritual breakthrough among the church members occurred when the American evangelist, Billy Graham, held a crusade in Haringey, London, each night except Sundays for a period of three months in 1954. The crusade commenced on 1st March with a total of two million people attending the meetings, including hundreds from all over North and South Wales.

Arrangements were made for a special train from North Wales to take interested people one Saturday to hear the evangelist. Starting at Holyhead, the express train stopped at the main stations to Chester and then proceeded non-stop to London. Among the hundred or more people waiting for the train at Holywell Junction was the author of this book. The 'Billy Graham train' was crowded! About twenty of the church members in Holywell Presbyterian Church professed faith in Christ that evening in addition to a few adherents. Having come to faith only a few months earlier in college, it was exciting for me to witness the immediate change in the ethos of the Holywell church the next day which was a Sunday. The church changed overnight, and for the better. But there was even more blessing in store for the church.

Glyn Owen[24]

Only six months later, the church was involved in extensive outreach in the locality and had invited the Rev. Glyn Owen to preach evangelistically each evening for a week, Monday to Saturday. Owen had been pastor of

---

24 Rev. Dr J. Glyn Owen (1919–2017) was born in Woodstock, Pembrokeshire. He trained for the ministry of the Presbyterian Church of Wales and ministered in Heath Presbyterian Church, Cardiff (1948–1954), Trinity Presbyterian Church, Wrexham (1954–1959), Berry Street Presbyterian Church, Belfast (1959–1969), and then succeeded Dr Martyn Lloyd-Jones as minister of Westminster Chapel, London (1969–1974) before moving to pastor Knox Presbyterian Church, Toronto, in 1974.

Heath Church, Cardiff, from 1948 to 1954 and only a few weeks earlier had moved to pastor Trinity Presbyterian Church in Wrexham. Owen preached powerfully each evening to growing congregations and by the end of the week over sixty people had been converted or had re-consecrated themselves. The church building was so full that it was decided to use the larger premises of the Welsh Presbyterian Church in the town for the final meeting on the Saturday evening. A number of Christians commented that 'the presence of God was even more striking on the final evening' and Owen remarked to those involved in inviting people to church that local people were hungry for God and the gospel. Holywell English Presbyterian Church was changed even more, with almost all its members professing conversion.

Wrexham

The Rev. Philip Eveson has provided a clear picture of the Lord's blessing in the Wrexham area during the 1940s and 1950s. He writes:

> *Glyn Owen moved from the Heath Church in Cardiff to Trinity Presbyterian Church, Wrexham, at the end of March 1954. He made it clear that he saw Trinity as an evangelical preaching centre. This had been the concern of the previous pastor, D. O. Calvin Thomas, whose ministry had begun just prior to the Second World War. Calvin Thomas had sought a church ... marked by a strong evangelical character ...,, the deepening of our spiritual life by searching the Scriptures and by faithfulness at the Means of Grace and the cultivation of a true fellowship of the Spirit. And during his time at Trinity (1954–1959) the numbers at the weekly prayer meetings increased and young adults were encouraged in their faith and commitment by the study of the Bible and the Westminster Shorter Catechism. Young people who were not able to attend the Tuesday evening church prayer meeting started their own each Wednesday morning at 8.15 before going to school or work. This carried on throughout Glyn Owen's time until the early 1960s. Philip Davies (later an elder in the Heath) and I were among*

those who attended in our teens before we went to university. Both my parents, newly married, were converted during the war under Calvin Thomas' early preaching ministry.

Special evangelistic activities began after the war with several campaigns organised; the one that was particularly blessed occurred in the spring of 1952. Additional prayer meetings were held every Saturday prior to the event and adverts appeared on the many cinema screens in the town. Every house in Wrexham was visited twice, once before the event to hand out invitations and the other afterward as a follow-up. Some of the housing areas had even been contacted earlier to encourage parents to send their children to Sunday School. The evangelist for the mission was David Shepherd from Gorseinon. I remember being amazed at the queues that gathered around the building to get into Trinity. It certainly more than matched those waiting to enter the cinemas! Lecture room, school room and the chapel itself were often packed to capacity. There were very noticeable results that seemed more permanent than previous efforts. These included a number of converts and those with clear evangelical beliefs attending the church and some became keen members. When Calvin Thomas began his ministry in 1938 there were 186 on the membership roll but by the time he left in 1953 there were 318. Numbers in Sunday School also rose substantially. I remember the fleet of Crosville buses that were required to take mothers and children on the annual summer outing to Rhyl. It seems that Calvin Thomas introduced to Trinity the practice that was common in many Welsh Presbyterian Churches of testing the meeting at the close of the evening service. An invitation was given to any who felt moved to commit themselves to Christ or to become members of the church, to stand. On many Sundays, people responded and prayer was offered for them and their names were recorded.

During the Shepherd campaign, meetings were also held in a number of the large coalmining villages around Wrexham, which *was an encouragement to earnest Christians in those localities. Some converted working-class men, concerned for the spiritual state of their district, engaged in evangelistic work that eventually led to the opening of the Rockwood Mission, Brynteg, in 1949 when Maynard James preached powerfully. One of the men then became concerned for the Coedpoeth area and soon a work was started in 1954 called the Adwy Mission. It was something that Winnie Davies, who had gone from her home in Coedpoeth to the Belgian Congo as a missionary with WEC, had been praying about for some years. On her first furlough, she was present for the opening meeting. She was killed by the Congo rebels in 1967.*

This was the background to Glyn Owen's call to Trinity, Wrexham. He too called the members to pray for the kind of spiritual power that had been known in earlier generations and certainly the prayer meetings were well attended. Following the Billy Graham Haringey Crusade in 1954 which affected many local people, the All-Scotland Crusade took place the following year in Kelvin Hall, Glasgow, and Graham's preaching was relayed to Trinity and each night from 19 to 30 April people crowded into the church, among them many young people. The following year, evangelistic services were held throughout October on Thursday, Saturday and Sunday evenings when members were encouraged to invite people along. These meetings were well-attended and it resulted in the Sunday evening services being packed throughout Mr Owen's ministry in Trinity. A trickle of soldiers stationed at the Royal Welsh Fusilier barracks in Wrexham attended and I have met a number in later years when visiting churches across Britain.

It was during Glyn Owen's time at Trinity that Mr Mawdsley, a Wrexham jeweller and member of Trinity, along with some of his family and young Christians from various churches who attended a Saturday evening fellowship that arose out of the Shepherd campaign, began holding open-air meetings at the Wrexham King

Street bus station near Trinity on a Sunday evening after church. It was a place where teddy boys would gather as well as interested girls and after the meeting some would accept an invitation to Trinity for light refreshments, a chat and a concluding message.

Glyn Owen informed me that one of his greatest joys and encouragements in Trinity was seeing so many of the young people converted and joining the church. Twenty-one of us were welcomed into the membership of the church on Easter Sunday 1958, the year before Glyn's departure for Berry Street, Belfast. I am in touch with some of them and know that they are still going on with the Lord.[25]

Mission Hall, Neath

The Mission Hall in Neath was yet another Forward Movement cause within the Presbyterian Church of Wales and has an interesting history. Early in the twentieth century, its ministers were Frank (1861–1920) and Seth Joshua (1858–1925), the latter having been used significantly in the 1904 revival and whose ministry was biblical and powerful.

I. B. Davies left Saltmead, Cardiff[26] and started his ministry in the Mission Hall in 1950 and the Rev. Andrew Davies, his younger son, comments on this period in his father's ministry. He writes, 'there were three groups in the congregation. Some were older Christians who had experienced the power of God during the 1904–05 revival' and it showed in their lives and praying:

There was a dimension to their praying and a sense of God about their living that was different. You knew that they knew God. There were others who had the right language but lacked reality. They were proud of the Mission but were unconverted. A smaller number had been influenced by the so-called higher criticism movement and had

---

25 The above material is based on Philip's own recollections and those of his father plus booklets and pamphlets of churches: Joan M. Hughes, *Trinity, A Town Centre Church* (1988); *Rockwood Mission 60th Anniversary 1949–2009*; *History of Coedpoeth Evangelical Church* (printout, 2000); David M. Davies, *The Captivity and Triumph of Winnie Davies* (London: Hodder & Stoughton, 1968).

26 See the previous chapter.

adopted liberal views of the Bible. They had replaced the gospel of grace by the 'social gospel' and were not slow to say so.

What happened? Some of the people were surprised by the preaching and ardour of their new minister. IB's

vigorous, direct, searching preaching began to sift the congregation. Some rejoiced, others protested. The choir sat behind the pulpit in full view of the congregation and their faces said it all. Throughout the twelve years of his ministry there was resistance to the preaching and the preacher.

The 'Tonna 6'[27]

While the opposition in the church remained and grew, 'at the same time remarkable things happened'. Andrew Davies continues the story:

Outsiders began to come in and many were converted. A group of rugby players heard that the new minister was keen on sport so they decided to go and hear him preach on a Sunday evening. They came again, compelled by what they were hearing. On Saturdays, they would gather in a pub after their rugby matches and discuss the previous week's sermon. Then they would be back for more. One by one they were converted.

The group of rugby players Andrew Davies refers to were known as the Tonna 6 and I am grateful to Mrs Marilyn Jeffreys, the daughter of Gwilym Edwards, one of the six, for providing me with valuable information from her relatives[28] and friends concerning these men. I am informed that the men included in this group were Gwilym Edwards and friend George Jenkins,

---

27 There is uncertainty as to whether there were six or seven. I have only been able to identify six names as belonging to the group.

28 Marilyn reports: 'Those who contributed are: Moira Evans & Eunice Walters, nieces of George Jenkins's wife, Olive; Shirley Rees, Mervyn's widow; Shirley Edwards, Bryn's widow; Janet Jones, Gwilym & Bryn's eldest niece; Myra, Gwilym's widow and their children Gareth Edwards & Marilyn Jeffreys. Most of these ladies are able to give first-hand accounts. Each of their faces have lit up as they recalled wonderful days in the Mission.'

Bryn Edwards and friend Idris Jones (Tonna), Mervyn Rees and Idris Jones (Cilfrew), who was called Little Id because of his stature and also Id Oil as he had a paraffin business after the war. Marilyn writes:

Like Gwilym, all served in the armed forces during WW2, Bryn in the Royal Navy and the rest in the army. They returned to Tonna scarred by what they had experienced during the war. Gwilym became a factory worker, Bryn a plasterer, George worked a milk round, Id (Cilfrew) had a business selling paraffin, while Id (Tonna) worked for BP. They were all hard-working men but their social lives centred on rugby, cricket and beer. Within the Tonna community, they were considered 'disruptive'. George was described as rough, anti-social, loud and reckless; Bryn was abrasive and argumentative, but they all drank to excess.

George Jenkins had been in the army in Burma, fighting the Japanese in hand-to-hand combat and was later awarded the Burma Star. Back at home he had settled into village life, became a regular at the Whittington Arms pub, like others, and for two years captained the Tonna rugby team. He became part of the close group of men, the Tonna 6, who were the scourge of the local Police Constable, Sam Williams, who often could not go to bed at night because of the group's 'mindless vandalism … Things usually happened after they had had a few pints'.

Let me introduce you to some of the men in more detail, beginning with brothers Gwilym and Bryn Edwards. Their mother was Bronwen Edwards (née Davies), who was born in Loughor in 1892 and came to faith in Christ during the 1904–05 revival.

She was a woman of prayer and her prayers were answered because all five children eventually came to faith, Gwilym and Bryn directly through the ministry of IB. From a young age, Bryn disliked Christianity and felt embarrassed when his mother sang hymns loudly while pegging clothes on the line outside. Bronwen was often heard praising God as she climbed the hill on the way home after buying groceries for the family. Bryn hated anything to do with the Bible and one day buried the family Bible in the garden! Being concerned that his nephews Gwilym and Bryn were wasting the lives that had been given back to them having survived six years of war service, Uncle Glyn Edwards, a 'bookie', told them to 'Stop ruining your lives. Go down and listen to that man in the Mission!'

John Thomas[29] describes the same incident:

One Friday night, something remarkable happened. For weeks previously, when they were rolling out of the Whittington Arms, a local bookie, an uncle to Gwilym and Bryn said, 'You lot of headers need to go down to hear that bloke in the Big Mission!' After a few weeks of this, George Jenkins snapped and responded: I've had a belly-full of you! I'll go on Sunday night to shut you up! Uncle Glyn, the bookie, incidentally, had no inclination to go with them himself. On the Sunday night, a crowd of them started attending the evening gospel services at the Mission Hall out of curiosity and for a laugh. They found the gospel message IB preached compelling, but on Mondays they returned to their usual life styles. Being aware of this sudden influx of young men who socialised in the Whittington Arms in Tonna, which was the base of Tonna Rugby Club at that time, IB urged those attending the church prayer meeting to 'pray for the men in the gallery'.

Joke

The pattern of attendance of these men continued for some time and it seemed to be a standing joke that they would sit in the front rows of the gallery and prepare to be battered by the preaching regarding their sinful lives and their need to repent. Although what was being

---

29 Notes of John Thomas, pastor of Lonlas Gospel Mission, Skewen, shared in George Jenkins' funeral on Friday 20 July 2001.

said was objectionable to them, they were being drawn by the Holy Spirit and their consciences were telling them that what he preached was right.

Discussing the sermon in the pub, they came under conviction of sin and in their own words they admitted, 'A terrible experience, we were under conviction and dangerous men.' George actually thought that someone in Tonna was telling IB all about them!

They were never put off by a lack of seating. On one occasion when there was an unusually large congregation present, they climbed above the ceilings of the two vestibules that led into the gallery and sat there! They might also turn up for an open-air meeting or a prayer meeting. They joined the Whitsun march of witness through the town but, as it was a very hot day, they dropped out at Victoria Gardens to grab a quick pint in the Queens Public House to quench their thirst. Unfortunately for them, IB spotted them and required them to stay behind at the recreational fields, where the churches met for games following the march, to clear the litter!

The men discussed the gospel while they downed their pints at the Whittington Arms and they were slowly facing up to the realisation that the Whittington Arms and the Christian faith were not compatible. Gwilym would challenge everyone as to what they were going to do with what they had heard, saying 'We can't go on like this, boys!'

It is believed that during 1952, Gwilym and George

were the first two Tonna boys to come to faith in the Lord Jesus, twelve years after Gwilym had made a promise on the beach at Dunkirk. He was in France when the Germans invaded in 1940 and spent days escaping on foot to the beach at Dunkirk. On arrival, he could barely see the sand because of the number of men on the beach, dead, dying and wounded, then cried out to God saying that if God would get him off the beach, he would serve Him for the rest of his life. Those words were uttered in June 1940. He and his mate eventually boarded a vessel and the next thing he knew was that they had berthed safely in England. Twelve years passed before Gwilym re-visited that promise made to a God he did not know.

Gwilym and George Edwards were gloriously converted but, despite continuing to attend the Mission, Gwilym's brother Bryn resisted the gospel. There was one occasion when he saw IB walking through town, preaching the gospel through a loudhailer. Rather than come face to face with him, Bryn darted into a shop, such was his conviction. There is another story about him struggling to lift his pint of beer to his mouth, feeling it was too heavy, such was the spiritual battle raging around him. Many months later, Bryn and Idris (Tonna) finally trusted the Lord. Not much is known about the circumstances save that when IB asked Bryn and Idris to accompany him to the vestry to pray, Bryn refused and knelt down at the front in the main hall and prayed the sinner's prayer where he was.

Bryn Edwards and Idris Jones were converted three months after the conversion of Gwilym and George.

Regarding Id (Cilfrew), he related many years later that he didn't think he needed to be saved, at least, not compared with the rest of the group! He described himself as 'self-righteous' but his eyes were opened although nothing is known now of the circumstances in which he was saved. Mervyn Rees was converted in 1954. He and his wife Shirley attended a Billy Graham Crusade in Haringey and it was at this event that Shirley became a Christian. Mervyn's conversion followed the very next day as a result of one of IB's sermons. When the community in Tonna heard of all these conversions, the men were mocked mercilessly and they were 'given six months', largely due to another Tonna man who, having made a commitment, abandoned his faith very quickly. He was henceforth called 'Dai the Liar' until the day he died.

Many Tonna men sat in the gallery in the Mission Hall but only a few responded. Despite the accusations and suspicions of the Tonna community, Gwilym, George, Bryn, Idris, Little Id and Mervyn stood firm in their faith. They were totally committed and faithful in their attendance on Sundays, the Monday night prayer meetings, the Bible studies, the open-air and some of them even joined the choir, although George was asked to leave due to his inability to sing in tune!

Changed lives

Gwilym and Bryn's eldest niece lived in the family home during this period and, though only 12–13 years of age, she knew that something was afoot. She said that previous to their conversion and during the Christmas break, the boys would have a party and the bath would be full of bottles of beer. That stopped! Bryn would invariably end up in a brawl outside the house having drunk too much and would fight on the rugby pitch too. The fights stopped as did the annual rugby trips to England and Scotland. In fact, on his first Christmas as a Christian, Bryn took his niece to a local department store and bought her a Christmas present. She couldn't believe it as previously he had never had money to buy her anything!

The men swapped their visits to the Whittington Arms for the MC Cafe near the bus station in Neath where they discussed the gospel over a coffee. The 'religious' people in Tonna are reported to have 'hated' the boys following their conversions and that never changed. A family member describes the change in George, post conversion, as 'a complete and wonderful transformation and deliverance'. A similar description could be applied to them all. Gwilym and Bryn's stepmother is recorded as saying that 'I never thought I would see the *day when Bryn would sit down and read the Bible!' Gwilym, Id and Mervyn were the quieter ones in the group, but George and Bryn's outgoing personalities were now directed at telling others how God had changed their lives.*

George's niece remembers him telling the family about one sunny day when a group of Jehovah's Witnesses knocked on doors in the terrace where they lived. George stood out the front, calling out to his neighbours that they should not listen to the JWs because they did not believe the gospel! Gwilym and Bryn shared their testimonies amongst family members and these were instrumental in a number of them coming to faith. On one occasion as IB was preaching in the open air in Neath, a pint of beer was thrown from an upper floor window of the Shakespeare Inn and only narrowly missing IB. George responded by shouting, 'You know, Wus, if I come up there, you'll come down quicker than you went up!'

Each of the men met their future wives through the Mission. Gwilym married Myra in 1954 and had two children. Despite IB's grave misgivings and advice to the contrary, due to Bryn's personality traits, Shirley married Bryn in 1956 and they were happily married for 54 years until Bryn's death in 2010. They had five children. Idris (Tonna) married Beryl and had four children; Mervyn married Shirley and they were blessed with two children, while George and Olive married in 1957.

Fruitful ministry

Regarding IB's ministry, the main thrust was to preach the gospel without any frills, both from the pulpit and on the streets. His burning desire was to see men, women and children saved and he is described as fearless in this pursuit. Someone is quoted as saying that, in this, the Mission was a battlefield. Those attending the Sunday services speak of the presence of the Spirit of God working and of people being saved most weeks. The place used to be packed out and the singing from the Sankey hymnal played a big part in the worship. One lady remembers IB's face beaming and full of joy as he sang 'I am redeemed. Oh praise the Lord!' To assist in the work, IB ran campaigns, inviting other like-minded men to preach. It is believed that Rev. Omri Jenkins spoke at one campaign for two weeks when fourteen people were saved.

IB's emphasis too was on prayer and he encouraged everyone to be present at, and participate in, the church prayer meetings. One person recalls the fact that her foot was gently nudged by IB's more than once if there was a lull in prayer, as if to say, 'Your turn. Get on with it. We're not here to twiddle our thumbs!'

However, despite the emphasis on preaching, IB was a very good pastor, displaying deep compassion, understanding and wisdom in his interaction with his flock. Shirley Rees recalls how wonderful IB was when she and Mervyn lost their first two babies, visiting them, running them to and then back from the hospital, supporting them in their grief. Shirley Edwards speaks of the time when he assisted with a very delicate situation within her parents' family, acting in a surprisingly non-judgemental way, wisely guiding them to a conclusion that brought great relief. He also nurtured his flock. He and 'Mrs IB' opened the doors of their home especially after the Sunday evening service.

The men testified to the presence and blessing of God in many of those services and though it was not revival yet they felt it was a 'taste' of what the Lord could do in revival. This group of men were known as' the Tonna boys' because they were from the nearby village of Tonna. They joined the church prayer meeting and began to pray out loud. Without having much of a biblical background, their prayers lacked biblical language but they were real and heartfelt prayers. They lifted the prayer meeting.

Neath fair

IB's ministry included open-air preaching where he was bold and direct. Andrew Davies refers to the annual September Fair in Neath where thousands of people gathered for the occasion 'so', he writes:

> IB galvanized people for action! The open-air meetings were nothing if not confrontational and electric. The new converts were encouraged to speak, receiving a great deal of abuse as they did so. But they also commanded a hearing. Beer was thrown at them. The greengrocer whose stall was next to the meeting pelted them with rotten fruit. On one of these occasions one of 'the Tonna boys' had had enough. He picked up the greengrocer with one hand and told him that if he continued with his abuse, he would get the other fist in his face. IB put his hand on his shoulder and said, 'George, you are in grace now!' But it did the trick!

In the Mission Hall,

> the number of new converts grew, including many young people, transforming the prayer meeting and swelling the congregation. Over a thousand people attended on a Sunday evening. The young people's meetings were especially memorable. Young people were asked to prepare talks and to articulate how they had been converted. This became the seed bed for the cultivation of future leaders.

'Something special'

Two incidents occurred which made a deep impression upon IB and both occurred in the annual evangelical ministers' conference at Cilgwyn. Cilgwyn was a Conference Centre in Newcastle Emlyn, a small agricultural town in south-west Wales. It was probably the 1957 or 1958 conference, when the tensions among the ministers relating to denominational differences, but also the Arminian and Calvinist divide, surfaced more obviously, with the divisions hardening into exclusive groups. One afternoon, Elwyn Davies reported that he went with others to a cafe for refreshments. Observing the Presbyterians sitting aloof from those of other denominations, he was embarrassed. When they returned in separate groups to the Centre, they all stood talking leisurely in the entrance foyer. Spontaneously, a circle was being formed. Suddenly, the informal talking gave way to spontaneous prayer when, within a few minutes, the Holy Spirit unexpectedly fell on them and gave them a great love for one another. Elwyn Davies describes what happened:

> *The Rev. I. B. Davies came to me and said, 'I love you brother' and I returned the same sentiment. Then all the other men also expressed their love for each other personally and genuinely.*

A deeper sense of unity and love between the ministers was experienced.[30] Andrew Davies reports that during 1959

> *something very special happened (in the church). For a period of six months the prayer meeting received an outpouring of the Holy Spirit. A sense of awe at the presence of God fell upon the gathering, so much so that those who arrived late were afraid to enter the room. Time seemed not to matter; prayer became free; the language of praise and petition became fluent and eloquent; Christ was pre-eminent. It was an extra-ordinary time. God was pleased to visit us and give us a little taste of what it must be like in a time of revival.*

It is significant that I. B. Davies was one of fifty or more pastors attending the Evangelical Ministers' Conference at Cilgwyn in June that year and that conference witnessed the 'most remarkable prayer meeting in the

---

30 D. Eryl Davies, *Dr Martyn Lloyd-Jones and Evangelicals in Wales: Bala Ministers' Conference 1955–2014* (Bridgend: Bryntirion Press, 2014), p. 77. This incident was described in detail to me by Elwyn Davies. However, Graham Harrison describes the same incident in more detail, adding that 'The men were literally laughing as a holy joy from the presence of God pervaded the place. It was an experience that meant much and taught much to those who were present … confirming the possibility of God drawing near to and blessing His people.' See *Contender for the Faith: a tribute to J. B. E. Thomas, Bethlehem, Sandfields* (Bridgend: Evangelical Movement of Wales, 1975), p. 17.

Conference's history.[31] Prayer was slow and heavy at first, so Lloyd-Jones intervened, rebuking the men for their discouraging prayers, navel gazing and lack of awareness in prayer of Christ's exalted glory. For Lloyd-Jones, the chief need of churches and preachers was to experience the Lord's presence and see his glory. It was a brief but powerful exhortation which led immediately to fervency and liberty in prayer with the elderly men touched in the 1904 revival taking the initiative. One minister commented:

> We were brought with a great sense of guilt in tears to the Saviour's feet ... The last prayers of the Conference were that God would make haste to show us his glory.[32]

There was a 'deep brokenness and honesty' in praying for an 'outpouring of the Spirit'. Men were not the same after that prayer meeting and all agreed that it was 'a foretaste of revival'. I. B. Davies himself was affected deeply by that prayer meeting and the church was to share in its blessing for a brief period.

Conflict

Nevertheless, this blessing was preparing the church for conflict. 'Not long afterwards (1962), opposition to the preacher and the preaching became strident and aggressive', writes Andrew Davies. 'Two years later IB was forced to resign and many of the new believers left to form a new evangelical congregation.'[33] It is impossible, however, to count the number of people who became Christians under IB's preaching of the gospel during this period.

During the 1970s I met several of the Tonna men who had been converted under IB's ministry in Neath. As we have illustrated, they were strong,

---

31 *Dr Martyn Lloyd-Jones and Evangelicals in Wales*, p. 86.

32 D. Eryl Davies, *Dr Martyn Lloyd-Jones and Evangelicals in Wales: Bala Ministers' Conference 1955-2014* (Bridgend, Bryntirion Press, 2014), pp. 86–87.

33 'Following IB's departure', writes Marilyn Jeffreys, 'George, Bryn and Idris (Tonna) settled at Lonlas Gospel Mission, Skewen, while Gwilym and Mervyn remained at the Mission, Mervyn until his untimely death at a relatively young age. Gwilym was appointed an elder and served faithfully until eventually he and Myra settled elsewhere. Little Id settled in Pisgah, a Welsh speaking Chapel in Cilfrew.'

colourful personalities with a story to tell, but full of the Lord. Rev. and Mrs I. B. Davies, after being ousted from the Mission Hall, Neath, in 1962, went that same year to New Zealand for a period to pastor a Presbyterian Church. Shirley Edwards has a photograph taken on Harwich railway station platform in 1962, showing some of the Tonna boys—Bryn, Gwilym and George—with IB as they were sending him and his family off to New Zealand.

In the next chapter we sample other ministries and churches in the 1960s.

Questions

1. How do you understand Elwyn Davies' explanation of blessing in his church, that 'a breeze from heaven passed by'?
2. Which aspects of blessing and conversions in the Holywell and Wrexham churches interest and challenge you?
3. What can we learn from prayer meetings in IB's church and in the Cilgwyn Conference for our own church prayer meetings today?

6. Wales 1950s – 1960s

We are lingering in the 1950s before turning to the 1960s in order to observe how, through the earnest preaching of the gospel and fervent prayer, many people were brought to faith in Christ. Some of the converts were already attending churches and were even church members, while others were unchurched, yet were brought savingly to Christ under gospel preaching. It is important to keep on remembering that what is written aims to *inform* churches concerning what God did in this period, then to *invite* Christians to think about the biblical principles underlying this period of blessing. Thirdly, the book seeks to *inspire* Christians and churches to pray fervently for the Lord to work powerfully in our contemporary situation.

We note again the close link between what God was doing in the colleges and its impact on some churches. The pastors referred to had recently left their respective colleges, and began to see conversions and spiritual growth as they settled into pastorates and evangelised. Before considering their ministries, we need to mention the unusual degree of blessing experienced in a student mission in the area of Cross Hands, Carmarthenshire, as one example.

Cross Hands

The Rev. H. H. Williams, known locally as 'HH', was a North Walian who had only recently accepted the pastorate of the Welsh Presbyterian Church in Cross Hands where a student mission was held in September 1952 and here, again, people were saved. The Rev. Gareth Davies was originally from the church and went on to pastor churches in Pontardawe, Llanelli and Ammanford, and he claimed that 'HH' was a key person during the period of blessing in the locality. 'HH' was short in stature, bald as well as lame and there was nothing attractive about his appearance or personality. However, he treasured and preached the gospel with passion so his local ministry was influential. He also nurtured young men like Gareth Davies and others who were called to the ministry. The Lord worked powerfully during this mission and afterwards. Eifion Evans, who was at that time a student training for the Christian ministry, preached one evening. He had little experience of preaching, but that evening he used a string of Bible texts underlining God's holy nature and the plight of people in sin and under God's wrath, before majoring on the divine remedy in the death of the Lord Jesus for sinners, then calling people to repent and trust in Christ. Those listening to him, refer to an unusual authority and power in the preaching.

From the late 1940s onwards, a significant number of young students from all over Wales trained for the preaching and pastoral ministry in 'liberal' denominational colleges, then were called to pastorates where they exercised useful biblical ministries over the following decades.

Gelli, Rhondda

The Rev. Hugh Morgan was from Llanelli and converted in 1945. After theological training, he was ordained and inducted to his first pastorate at Bethany Presbyterian Church in Gelli, a heavily populated mining area in the Rhondda Valley, where he served for nine years until 1962. An elder in Bethany, Dilwyn Jones, referred to the situation when Hugh Morgan became their pastor in 1953:

> At that time, the members were religious, and only a few professed conversion … It was not easy for the minister, for some were resentful, unwilling to acknowledge that they were sinners in the sight of God.

Derek Swann confirmed that when Hugh arrived there,

> the situation was bleak … Concerts and sales of work were used to augment church funds. Hugh set about preaching repentance and faith in Christ and, despite resentment and an unwillingness to be told they were sinners, hearts were melted and people were saved.

The Bible became central to the life of the church and true spiritual life began to flourish. He is remembered with great affection among his people to this day.

A good number of local people were converted under Hugh's preaching ministry so that Bethany became a warm, loving fellowship where the Lord was honoured. There was considerable blessing and growth in the church, which greatly encouraged Hugh and his wife Mari. Hugh also attended the Evangelical Ministers' Conference at Cilgwyn in 1959 at which he, like many of the ministers present, was greatly affected by the final prayer meeting.[34]

Over the following months, Hugh wanted to pray for hours rather than minutes each day and the result was considerable blessing in the church at Gelli. Hugh's widow, Mari, informed me that neither she nor Hugh wanted to leave Gelli for they loved the people and had become very attached to them and especially because considerable blessing was being experienced in the pastorate. Nevertheless, Hugh agreed to preach in Malpas Road Church, Newport, knowing they were looking for a pastor. On his first preaching visit to the church, members of the Pastorate Committee were not impressed with his preaching, but providentially in their next meeting, and following the fervent prayer of some committee members, they agreed to extend a call to him. Before long, Hugh felt the compelling call of the Holy Spirit that he should accept the invitation. His induction service was held in November 1962 but 'there were great tears of emotion among the Gelli members in the loss of their minister'.[35]

Malpas Road, Newport, Gwent

The Church had been established by the Forward Movement and when Hugh Morgan began his thirty years of ministry there, the church membership was 350 but attendance at the Sunday services was only about 40. Gerald

---

34 See chapter 5 under 'Something special'.
35 I am grateful to Gerald Pontin for permission to quote him for he has researched this period of the church's history.

Pontin reports that Hugh recognised that there had been an over-emphasis on the social aspects of church life, which served to blur the church's vision of the gospel. Howard P. Miles declares that the church in 1962 'knew little of gospel light and hope … and there were many things in those days to clutter up that vision' [36] which Hugh Morgan had of preaching the gospel. 'He knew the task that faced him—the task of preaching the gospel.'

A significant number of people were removed from the membership roll due to non-attendance and more were removed during the following three years so that at the start of 1965 there were 218 on the roll instead of 350. There was also opposition to Hugh's ministry. Over the next years as people were converted and others moved into the area or joined from other local churches, non-attendees were removed from the membership so that at the beginning of 1972 the membership was 221, peaking at 267 in early 1987. Hugh and Mari were very concerned in the first two years of ministry at Malpas Road as there seemed to be a lack of spiritual fruit and conversions, but they received a rebuke from the Lord. On their way home from a wedding in Kent, one couple who had joined the membership of the church when they were teenagers shared with them that they had recently come to faith in the Lord Jesus Christ under Hugh's ministry. Hugh and Mari felt God had reprimanded them because they did not believe he was working and they vowed after that experience never again to doubt that he was always at work. Nevertheless, the first few years were difficult because changes were being made in imposing a New Testament pattern on the church, with the emphases being placed on prayer, preaching, evangelism and mission.

On Sunday, in addition to the morning and evening services, there were the afternoon Senior Sunday School, Primary Sunday School and Adult Men's and Ladies' Bible Classes. The activities of the church, including the children's and youth works, needed to be brought under one umbrella, with the YPF meeting after the Sunday evening service. Not all those involved

---

36 'A good minister of Jesus Christ: Hugh David Morgan, 1928–1992' (*Evangelical Magazine of Wales*, April/May, 1992), pp. 5–8. The quotations from Howard Miles, Derek Swann, Peter Milsom and Gwilym Roberts are taken from this issue.

in leading the groups were happy with the new arrangements. The average number of scholars attending in 1963 was 120 which rose to 210 by 1976. Hugh and Mari started adult Bible classes in the sixties when attendance was in single figures, but by 1976 the men's class had about fifteen regular attendees and the ladies' forty-one. The only way to obtain adequate space and rooms for this developing work was to build, in 1982, a first floor on the church hall containing additional classrooms. The growth of the children's work was encouraging; as parents were converted, they brought their children to Sunday School and the youth meetings in the week flourished with well over 150 attending. Many young people, once they were converted, wanted to be helpers in church activities. Separate evangelistic meetings for men and women were held periodically and guest services were held on some Sundays to which people were encouraged to bring their friends.

Prayer

Howard Miles had no hesitation in describing Hugh Morgan as

> *a man of prayer. He confessed on many occasions that he often found prayer hard—the hardest part of his ministry. Yet, because it was so hard, he prayed all the more, and he urged us to pray … The great burden on his heart was to see a day when God would come again and visit his people. It was a burden he had from his earliest days. How appropriate that at the Saturday morning prayer meeting for revival at 7.00 am Hugh Morgan was there, and then just after 9.00 am when he reached home, he was taken home to glory.*

For Hugh, the prayer meeting was the power house of the church and therefore the most important meeting, so everyone was encouraged to make this meeting a priority. An attendance of about twenty-five in the sixties had increased to about eighty every week by the mid-seventies. All church officers and new converts were encouraged to attend and also to pray for revival. Men were encouraged to set up family worship in their homes and, whenever possible, encouraged the remainder of the family to take part in reading the Bible, discussion and prayer. In 1968 there was an election of elders, bringing their number up to fifteen and in May 1969 pastoral visitation by elders in pairs to members and adherents was introduced, which proved beneficial, with the elders required to report back at their next meeting. This new arrangement united the members even more and brought considerable encouragement. The late sixties showed some improvement in the spiritual life of the church with a few conversions, but what happened in the seventies was remarkable, and many would say a mini-revival was experienced.

In February 1972, the minister and an elder, Gerald Pontin, visited Stornoway in the Western Isles of Scotland because God had recently visited his people in revival and they were interested to know what had happened. The secret, they discovered, was believing prayer that God would answer if his people humbled themselves and called upon his name to revive them. It really was a taste of heaven upon earth for Hugh and his companion and they returned thrilled at what they had heard and seen and encouraged the church to pray likewise. Gwilym Roberts reminds us that prayer, for Hugh, was not something recent or spasmodic, but rather from his student days in the theological college in Aberystwyth he was a regular member of the prayer group.

> *He had a deep conviction regarding the need of prayer, and the value of believers meeting to pray for the Lord of the harvest to thrust forth labourers into his harvest and to pour out his Spirit in revival upon his people in our land.*

Burden

It is no surprise, then, that in 1965, three men in the Malpas Road Church, including Hugh Morgan and Gerald Pontin, shared a burden for revival. The three men agreed to meet for prayer for two hours on a Saturday morning, initially from 6.00–8.00 am, which was subsequently re-arranged for a slightly later time of 7.00–9.00 am. Reporting in the Church Magazine of

Spring 1972 shortly after returning from the Isle of Lewis, Gerald gave their reasons for going there. One reason was 'to acquire a first-hand account of what God is doing there, then see and hear about some of the supernatural workings of God'. They also wanted assurance that as a church in Newport they were 'moving in the right direction to obtain God's blessing'. In fact, '… it was a wonderful experience, meeting with a revived people of God, something I shall never forget.' Gerald then shared some lessons which 'were becoming very clear', including the need to trust God and believe what he says in the Bible; living lives of prayer; praying for revival; the importance of family worship and living lives consistent with the Bible. He concluded, 'I believe that God can work in such a way here in our church …'

The minister himself wrote an editorial in the same issue explaining that 'our theme of this Magazine is Revival'. He explained, 'Revival is the great need of the church today.' Referring to Psalm 44, he emphasised that hearing and reading about revivals '… will create within us a desire to see God's Spirit being poured forth once again upon this land of ours'. He added:

> Revival always brings great glory to God, for a revived church is a God-glorifying church … it is therefore essential that the people of God should consider this whole question of a quickening within the church. Let us ask God to give us as a church prayer for revival.

In the same church magazine, Philip Eveson wrote briefly on 'The Biblical Teaching on Revival'.[37]

Apart from sickness or holiday, the group of men who had started meeting to pray for revival from 1965 continued to meet every Saturday until 1975 when additional elders were elected. The day was then changed to Friday and the time from 10.00 pm until midnight was chosen for their prayer meeting at the church. In later years, monthly area prayer groups were set up in members' homes, chaired by an elder, to help people take part in discussion and to pray in smaller groups, as many found the size of the church prayer

---

37 This is included in the Appendix.

meeting overpowering. A week of prayer was also held at the beginning of each year.

For two years, between 1971 and 1973, the Rev. Philip Eveson and his wife Jenny attended the church. Philip had been called as minister to the dual pastorate of Havelock Street Presbyterian Church, Newport, and Bethania, St Mellons. He resigned along with other evangelical ministers over the denomination's drive to support the unbiblical ecumenical movement and its liberal theological position. His own church at Havelock Street supported the denomination and opposed his evangelical stance. Philip writes, 'Hugh and Mari Morgan were most kind to us and we praise the Lord for those years there.' He later wrote, 'The two-year period we spent in Malpas Road was wonderfully uplifting and beneficial for Jenny and me after the three difficult years in Havelock Street' where, in the final months, there was 'anger and hatred' from some members.

> God was clearly at work in Malpas Road Church and had transformed the lives of a number of families. I recall the moving times of prayer at the early Saturday morning elders' prayer times. The eldership was made up of a number of men who had been converted or had grown theologically robust under Hugh's ministry. Hugh was encouraged by five younger men who became elders in 1968 … four had grown up in the church. There was much earnest praying for revival and there were some very special times of prayer. Hugh was also very wise in his dealings in the elders' meetings.[38]

Preaching

Preaching the gospel was very important for Hugh Morgan and he had been given the gift of presenting the truth clearly and in a very challenging way. He was gifted in expository preaching and the Holy Spirit was certainly at work, especially in the 1970s when congregations increased, conversions were frequent and almost every week someone came to faith. It has been

---

38 Emails, 8 February 2021 and 10 May 2021.

estimated that over 130 people came to faith in the sixties, seventies and early eighties.

There were some conversions in the 1960s, probably about ten, but during the 1970s about fifty-six were converted, including Peter Baker's parents. At the time, Glyn Baker was headmaster of St Julian's comprehensive school in Newport and became a church elder later in 1975. Eight young people including Peter Baker[39] and his future wife Sian Morgan, Hugh's younger daughter, became members in January 1973, then during the 1980s about fifty-seven, with another ten converted in the early 1990s up to Hugh Morgan's death in February 1992.

The Lord had been dealing with Bruce Powell,[40] the son of a church elder, prior to Hugh commencing his ministry in Malpas Road. Bruce's brother, Stuart, and his wife were already church members but came to understand the truth of the gospel and believe personally on the Lord Jesus Christ. That had been true of Bruce's father while his mother was converted later. Philip Eveson reports that 'adherents and young people were also being converted and joining the church on a regular basis each month' while he was in the church.

One thrilling encouragement was the conversions that took place through personal evangelism, as many people could tell of someone in their family who had been converted. An unconverted lady, who was a member of the church, and her husband were friendly with another couple and whenever the four of them met they often discussed the Bible. One of the husbands became irritated when the other lady quoted statements she had heard from the preaching of Hugh Morgan and vowed that he would attend church to sort those people out. He went to the men's Bible class and the sorting out did take place, with both couples being converted. Each couple had two children who were also converted afterwards. One exciting fact is that from an initially unconverted church member there were as many as fifteen relatives who were brought to faith in Christ!

---

39 Peter Baker became minister of Highfields, Cardiff and then Lansdowne Road, Bournemouth.
40 After later training for the ministry at London Bible College, he had various pastorates including Castle Street, Tredegar.

In 1967, a young couple who moved into the Malpas area attended church and were converted. The wife brought along her sister, who had lost her husband in a terrible car crash, to hear the gospel and she was saved in 1973. She re-married a non-Christian but brought him to church; he himself was then converted early in 1975. The sibling's brother, with his wife, visited them from Australia in 1974. He, too, was saved in October and his wife later in December while reading the Scriptures at a motorway service station on the way to London Airport for their flight home.

In 1976 the church seceded from the Presbyterian Church of Wales to become Malpas Road Evangelical Church, but church unity was maintained. 'The period of unusual blessing when God visited us in Malpas Road Church will be remembered for many years. We called upon his name,' writes Gerald Pontin, and

He heard and answered. He sent the blessing and many will be thankful for the change that took place in their lives and their families. Those days will never be forgotten. Such days of blessing can return but by prayer, preaching of the gospel, personal evangelism, ensuring that our families, friends, relations and work colleagues hear the news that Jesus Christ died on the cross for sinful people like ourselves. May God give us a burden for the lost and belief that he can send revival. That is what the church needs today.

At Hugh's funeral service, some words written by Evan Roberts in 1905 during the Welsh Revival were read out by Howard Miles. These words had been important for Hugh Morgan:

Holy Spirit, purify and possess everything for Thy glory and keep me to the end, if end there be, in Thy service. Teach me to serve. Let me not tire of serving. Give me the pleasure of serving. Teach me to bend as low as I would desire to go, as low as Thou the most holy and righteous Being, would have me go. Open my eyes to see work. Fill my heart which will be cleansed by Thee for work. Direct my paths towards work; not my work but Thy work. Keep my fingers clean from contaminating Thy work, the work which cost divine blood, work sanctified by sweat, yes, by tears, yes, by the blood of my God's heart. Work, with all the riches of the Godhead in it ... So, my God, draw me to Thy work, keep me in Thy work; let Thy work keep me, and keep me able to draw others into Thy work. Own Thy work these days; own Thy work for the sake of the atonement, and remember the intercession of Thy Son, Thy holy Son Jesus, and Thy sons Thy servants. Baptize me with work for the sake of the Great Worker.

These words express well the desires and love of Hugh Morgan for the Lord and the work of his kingdom. Hugh had given himself to one who had given himself sacrificially that we might be saved. He felt it was a huge privilege, therefore, to give himself wholly to the Lord and to his work.

Questions

1. Are there any significant features of God's work in Cross Hands and in Gelli, Rhondda, which are important and relevant today?
2. Does the continuing emphasis on prayer in Hugh Morgan's ministry in Gelli and Newport present us with both personal and church challenges?
3. How significant do you think the visit to Stornoway in the Isle of Lewis by the pastor and an elder was for the Newport church?

7. Pembrokeshire— Evangelism and Conversions

This is by no means an exhaustive account of the Lord's blessing in Pembrokeshire but a small sample of what God did in the county.

Cosheston mission

Cosheston is a small village situated close to the historic town of Pembroke in south-west Wales. Here again the Lord worked unexpectedly in blessing over a brief period. The leaders of Beulah Mission in Aberdare were keen to spread the gospel message and prayerfully seized the initiative in starting evangelistic preaching meetings in Cosheston for a week in both spring and autumn for a number of years. They decided to hold the meetings in an old unused chapel building in the village. No services or meetings were being held in the building either during the week or on Sundays. Stuart Olyott, who knew the place well, described it as 'a damp building without electricity, hidden away at the end of a short lane'. In recent years 'the lane has been surfaced and there is a car park at the end. The building has been extended to include a schoolroom, study, kitchen and toilets. It has a damp course, electricity, heating and double glazing,'[41] but there was nothing attractive about the building in the 1960s.

The first week of evangelistic meetings was held with Emrys Davies of Mount Pleasant Baptist Church, Swansea, preaching in March and the evangelist Idris Davies, Ammanford, preaching in the autumn. Attendances were encouraging and the preaching was well received.

---

41 Stuart Olyott, *Something Must Be Known & Felt: A Missing Note in Today's Christianity* (Bridgend: Bryntirion Press, 2014), pp. 8–10.

Hywel Griffiths

Rev. Hywel Griffiths, a former coal-miner, who pastored Litchard Mission in Bridgend, was responsible for a week of preaching in 1962, and preached in Cosheston each year until 1967. His ministry was powerful and signally used of God to deal with both believers and unbelievers. One of the young people who attended these meetings was Rowland Hicks, who was not a Christian when Griffiths began his visits. He relates his impressions of the preacher and his preaching:

> Hywel Griffiths stayed in our home during the week of preaching and he became one of the family. The services began at 7.30 pm each evening and Hywel Griffiths preached for about forty minutes. At the end of each service, no one moved or spoke and this went on for about fifteen minutes when spontaneously someone would pray or read some Bible verses or announce a hymn to be sung. The Lord's presence was so real and overwhelming that no one wanted to go home. A few minutes after 10.00 pm, the meeting would be ended. Although I was not a Christian at the time, the Lord was present and there was something special in the meetings.

Hicks refers to the week of preaching meetings in 1967 when Hywel Griffiths preached on the words of the Apostle Paul in 1 Thessalonians 5:21: 'Hold fast what is good'. Soon after the service ended, about twenty of the young people left to attend a Christian conference in Filey. Hicks was converted at that sea-side resort when John Blanchard preached on the words of 2 Corinthians 5:17: 'Therefore if anyone is in Christ, he is a new creation.'

Conversions

During this period, Hicks says that about fifteen young people trusted in Christ, with others returning to the Lord after a period of backsliding and compromise. He insists that it is impossible to know how many people were either converted or blessed and restored through the ministry of Hywel

Griffiths because all those in the services worshipped in different churches on Sundays so follow-up was difficult.

The Olyott family became residents in the village during the 1960s and it was Stuart Olyott's father who suggested they should start a Sunday service in Cosheston. That is what happened and after a few months they began to hold Sunday morning services and then later, evening ones as well. Stuart describes the background, together with his own impressions of the preaching of Hywel Griffiths and its impact on him. Stuart was training for the ministry at the time in London and so was unable to hear Hywel Griffiths when he first preached in Cosheston in 1962. His mother, however, was impressed by the preaching, claiming 'there was something about Hywel that could not be put into words ... All she could tell me was that it was wonderful.' A year later, Stuart was present to hear Hywel Griffiths preach throughout the week and he takes up the story:

> *Hywel Griffiths preached lengthily, filled his sermons with word pictures, clearly felt in his soul the truths he was proclaiming, and poured out his love for everyone present.*

But there was more, for there

> *was an indefinable influence ... heaven came to earth. Another voice was heard ... There was a touch of glory ...*

Stuart was not alone in feeling like that because all in the congregation were

> *overcome by the sheer power of the Word. Sometimes the silence was followed by spontaneous prayer, where one and another cried out to the Lord, wept their way to the cross, or renewed their vows to love him and to live for him. And I, like many others, was changed for ever. We had experienced a small taste of what happens in revival.*[42]

---

42 *Something Must Be Known & Felt*, pp. 9–10.

Norman Ellison[43]

In 1954, at the age of forty, Norman Ellison was led from Emmanuel Bible College in Birkenhead, Merseyside, into Pembrokeshire to engage in evangelism, which he did for twenty-seven years and without any salary. Hailing from Yorkshire and having worked for years in a Yorkshire coal-mine, he and his wife, were eager to serve the Lord. Initially he was called to work in Solva, a tiny village harbour, to lead the outreach in a small Presbyterian church building which had been closed for two years and only infrequently used. He held a Sunday evening service at 7.30 pm so as not to compete with other churches, and a small number of people were converted through his ministry there. His sacrificial lifestyle and love endeared him to the people, with both English and Welsh speaking people respecting him. In 1956, he moved with his wife to a flat in St David's and began to widen his evangelistic outreach by starting a children's work. Between 1954 and 1960, he held thirty-one missions in towns and villages throughout the county, with sixty-one other outlying areas visited from his central location by 1967. Each home would have been systematically visited twice in order to reach people with the gospel.

Three-week beach missions were also held annually in Saundersfoot, Pendine, Newquay and Tenby, with children, young people and parents being responsive. A considerable amount of sowing of the Word took place during Ellison's ministry, with a harvest of people coming to faith, even after his death. He estimated that his evangelism had covered about 70 per cent of the county of Pembrokeshire, accompanied by considerable pastoral work. From 1961–67, a caravan was adapted into a mobile church to seat thirty people, which proved popular and useful. The custom was for the mobile church to be parked centrally in villages near playing fields as the following story illustrates.

---

43 I am indebted to the Rev. John Welsby for this information. It was a privilege to supervise John's MA dissertation on the life and ministry of the Rev. Norman Ellison (1914–1981) in Pembrokeshire on behalf of Union School of Theology. His dissertation was approved by the University of Wales in 2007. This work deserves to be made available to the public.

1964 mission

In 1962, Peter Trumper (1934–2015) commenced his ministry in two Presbyterian churches, in Wiston and Goshen. Both he and Norman Ellison were burdened for evangelism and decided to hold a mission in Clarbeston Road in February 1964, using the mobile church as the venue for the meetings. Originally planned for two weeks, the mission continued for three months, with meetings each evening, and people 'professed faith in Christ ... forty for the six weeks of the mission'.[44] Trumper himself refers to this period as a 'period of blessing' despite tensions within his pastorate and disagreement with Ellison's 'holiness' teaching. Eighteen months after the mission ended, an unused Presbyterian church building in the village was opened, with a notice declaring 'Penuel Preaching Centre'. Soon, there was the remarkable provision of land and gifts to build a church, which became Bethany Free Church in Clarbeston Road.

Questions

1. Many children, young people and adults heard the gospel in Pembrokeshire over these years. Are there lessons and challenges for us today from their evangelism?
2. What do you think lies behind the effective preaching of the gospel in Cosheston?
3. How ready are we to reach out into the community with the gospel?

---

44 Peter Trumper, *As Far as to Bethany: A personal view of a remarkable period: 1962–1970* (Vocal Protestants' International Fellowship, 2000).

8. Blessing in Maesteg

Bethlehem Presbyterian Church was located in the attractive Llynfi valley town of Maesteg, with its population of almost thirty thousand people. Three coal mines dominated this open and attractive valley. An increasing number of men had begun to work in the large steel works in Port Talbot, while several small factories had opened in the town by the early sixties. Bethlehem Church was outwardly prospering in the late 1950s and early 1960s, with an active membership of well over 200 people with a good cross-section of ages. There was a large youth fellowship, attended by over a hundred between the ages of fifteen to the mid-twenties and a Sunday School with more than 150 children. A number of the young people were marrying and starting families and the church's future seemed bright. The church was well organised with twelve church elders, including three women. Two of the men belonged to secret organisations like freemasonry and a working-class equivalent. Despite the active and large membership of the church, with its well-attended Sunday evening service, there were very few converted members and only about two elders had a clear testimony to God's saving grace in Christ.

Positive

A major decision had been made in 1958 by the church elders to stop holding jumble sales and concerts to boost church income. The reasons were not biblical, but factors like friction and disagreement amongst the organisers contributed to the decision. The church situation in one sense looked attractive. The church had been without a minister for over ten years due to the shortage of ministers and to the denominational ruling which limited the number of pastors each Presbytery was allowed to have. Superficially at least, the church had prospered exceptionally well although it was eager to have a pastor. One major problem was that the church had imbibed liberal and critical views of the Bible from previous pastors and visiting preachers over several decades, resulting in confusion amongst members and the youth regarding what they believed. Most people considered the Old Testament unreliable and the miracles of Jesus, although interesting stories for children, not necessarily historical. Many were also ignorant of the gospel message, with one church elder reading from a Jehovah Witness' book occasionally in the weekly prayer meeting! No one suspected that book was heretical and unbiblical.

The above description of Bethlehem Church is typical of many other denominational churches in the period. Apart from a handful of church members with a clear testimony to God's grace in Christ, the vast majority of people in the church were sincere but very nominal in their profession of faith, yet loyal to the church. One woman elder, Mrs Thomas, Clara Towy and her missionary daughter, Marion, serving with the Red Sea Mission Team as a nurse in the Yemen, had devoted themselves to praying over a long period for an evangelical minister to be called to the pastorate. Their prayers were eventually answered in late 1959.

Trinity, Nantyffyllon

In the Lord's providence, a smaller Presbyterian church, Trinity, in the mining village of Nantyffyllon in the same valley and located about two miles from Bethlehem, had enjoyed a succession of student pastors most summers during the 1950s. The students were candidates for the Presbyterian ministry and studying theology in the denominational theological college in Aberystwyth. Some of these student pastors included John Thomas who became pastor of Sandfields, Aberavon and Gwilym Roberts, who later served churches in Tredegar, Holywell and Caergwrle, Wrexham. For two successive summers, I myself was invited to serve Trinity as student pastor and it was a rich experience. In a pastor-less church like Trinity, I gained invaluable experience in providing consecutive preaching on Sundays, leading Bible studies and prayer meetings, assuming responsibility for the youth work, attending elders' meetings and engaging in full pastoral visitation, as well as evangelism. I cannot thank folk at Trinity Church enough for their love and the freedom given me to lead the work, as well as to learn so much from them. This was pastoral training at its best and in the raw.

One afternoon, after visiting the local hospital, I walked to the top of a small mountain nearby as I needed to prepare sermons and spend time in prayer. I sat on the grass on a warm sunny day looking down on the Llynfi Valley. During the hours spent there, I received an inward but powerful conviction that one day I would pastor the large Bethlehem Church. This was a shock to me as Trinity Church had little contact with Bethlehem and the larger church did not know me. However, I was given a deep love for the people in the valley. Bethlehem Church knew that, despite its large membership, they were not allowed by the Glamorgan West Presbytery to have an ordained minister, yet early in 1959 they were informed that they could call a student who was completing his training. The other condition was that they had to form a joint pastorate with the smaller church, Trinity, with its fifty or more members. Trinity Church was thrilled at the prospect and eventually there was agreement between the two churches. By April 1959, after preaching in Bethlehem for the first time as a final year candidate for the ministry, I received a call to become the pastor.

Difficult

Newly married, I majored on preaching the gospel and caring pastorally for the people in both churches, but the narrative is now narrowed down to Bethlehem Church in an attempt to describe what the Lord did.

The first six years of ministry were difficult, with the church elders initially not allowing a weekly Bible study. Many members had no interest in the gospel, despite attending the Sunday evening service and respecting the pastor. There were discouragements galore. One major disappointment was that the senior church elder led a second meeting following the evening preaching service. This had been a custom in many churches for decades in order to 'test' whether people were affected by the preaching and wanted to 'respond.' What the elder did in fact was to disagree with what I had preached and this continued for at least two years. Despite my preaching and pastoral work, the response to the gospel was disappointing, although a small number of younger people came to personal faith in the Lord Jesus Christ.

The Lord's dealings

After nearly seven years, I felt more desperate and dependent on the Lord, convinced that only he could change what was humanly speaking an impossible church situation. This conviction grew, strengthened by fellowship with colleagues in the monthly Evangelical Ministers' Fraternal held in Sandfields Church, Port Talbot. One Monday in early 1966, following a helpful morning Bible study and time of prayer in the ministers' fraternal, we agreed to stay on until the afternoon to share pastoral and personal concerns before spending more time in prayer. It was an encouraging and heart-warming time, marked by a united longing amongst the ministers to know the Lord better and to see him work more powerfully in our churches. The Lord's words to the church in Laodicea in Revelation 3:20 were referred to and discussed, with the picture of the living Christ standing on the edge of our churches and also our personal lives, but calling pastors and Christians to closer, more intimate fellowship with him. We pastors returned home deeply challenged, but encouraged and hopeful.

Luke 11:1–13

That Monday evening, I led the weekly prayer meeting in the smaller Trinity Church in Nantyffyllon and read from Luke 11:1–13. As I read those verses, it seemed as if the Lord emblazoned the verses on the wall in front of me and I stared in amazement at the verses for seconds, although it seemed longer. I do not know until this day whether the verses were actually inscribed on the wall or not, but it seemed as if they were and my eyes were transfixed on words like 'Ask … seek … knock…'

How could I know the Lord better? I saw the answer in those words. 'Ask— that seemed easy enough, but such asking involved seeking too. I also knew that the verb 'seek' was the same word used by the Lord Jesus when he said he had come to 'seek and save that which was lost' (Luke 19:10). This verb indicates that the Lord's mission involved great effort, obedience and sacrifice. Then there was the challenge to 'knock' and persist in knocking. But could someone like me, a young pastor, know the Lord better and know the power of the Holy Spirit personally and in ministry? Could Bethlehem Church be changed? After all, I was not in the same league as men in previous revivals in Wales, like Howell Harris and Daniel Rowland, or George Whitefield in England or, more recently, the well-known preacher Dr Martyn Lloyd-Jones. Then my eyes were riveted on the word *everyone* in Luke 11:10, and I knew with immediate assurance that I myself was included, although I was amazed at the possibility, but excited too. The Lord's words indicating the generosity and willingness of the Father to give the Holy Spirit also struck me powerfully: *'how much more'* kind and generous is God the Father. Yes, though sinful fathers can give good gifts to their own children, *'how much more'* will our loving heavenly Father 'give the Holy Spirit to them that ask him.'

Prayer

To say that I was stunned by these verses would be an understatement. Nevertheless, the prayer meeting carried on as normal in its slow and tedious manner. My wife and I returned home, but God had spoken in his Word. Later that evening I received an unexpected phone call from a pastor colleague whom I had not seen for months and who knew nothing of my longings at the time. That colleague was the Rev. Vernon Higham in Cardiff, who invited me to spend the next day with him in prayer and in the Word from 8.00 am onwards. That is what happened and the hours spent in prayer were encouraging, but in the late afternoon the Lord met with us both, his presence becoming overwhelmingly real and awesome.

'Reality'

How does one describe that moment? It is very difficult even to try and explain what happened. Words and phrases like 'reality', 'warmth', 'humbling', 'an overwhelming awareness of God,' 'brokenness' and 'like a magnet being drawn closer to the Lord' are inadequate to describe what actually happened. Words fail to describe or capture the depth and reality of the experience. But the Lord had met with us.

That evening I was leading the church prayer meeting in Bethlehem, which usually was a hard, dismal affair, with few real prayers. I tried to share what had happened earlier, but within seconds it was impossible to carry on and so my wife added a brief explanation before the prayer time started. There seemed outwardly to have been no impact on the meeting as it took its normal course of long periods of silence, the reading of hymns and even prayers. However, when the meeting closed all was different and on their way out, individuals were close to tears or crying. Middle-aged women, hardened to the gospel, began to tell me as they left words like, 'I feel dirty'. Some of the coal miners held my hand tightly, saying, 'I'm going home to pray,' while others, emotionally moved, shook my hands firmly, unable to say anything. Knowing the people and their indifference, as well as their hardness to the gospel over the previous years, it was incredible and surprising to see the change in their attitudes. I had not done anything different at all in my ministry, except pray more and become gripped by the power of the Lord's promises.

The Lord at work

How does one describe what the Lord did over the following months? Again, words are inadequate. All I knew was that I was a spectator and was greatly surprised time and time again at what the Lord was doing in saving church members of all ages, recalling backsliders to himself and bringing outsiders into his kingdom. I was the same average preacher, but the Lord accompanied the preaching with a greater degree of authority and power. Only God could have done it. Weeks later, on a Sunday evening, and following a week in Bala, serving as a chaplain for young teens, the text of 1 John 1:5–7 and its message was given to me immediately prior to the service, and I became aware even of listening to my own preaching and, like others, being challenged by it.

On another occasion, a deacon, Ieuan Evans, joined me as we counselled a man who had been involved in the occult. It was a difficult session, with considerable hardness and resistance on the man's part, but then, unexpectedly, Ieuan was given 'holy laughter' in prayer as he rejoiced in God's mighty power and the glorious victory of Christ on the cross over sin, death and the devil. I had never heard such powerful, believing prayer before and have not heard such praying since. There was no question that God could save the man and I was amazed that a shy, unassuming, godly man like Ieuan was given such freedom and boldness in prayer. The man in question protested and shouted, moving around the church hall, throwing chairs around as he expressed anger, ordering Ieuan to stop praying like that. That prayer was 'in the Spirit' and God's presence and power were awesome. Months later the man was saved.

Sovereign

The awareness of the Lord's sovereignty in the situation was striking. The sowing of the Word in the church over the previous six years had been crucial. That was the Lord's revealed will because 'faith comes by hearing, and hearing by the Word of God' (Romans 10:17). I had been sent there too, in unusual circumstances, by the Lord, 'for how shall they believe in him of whom they have not heard? And how shall they hear without a preacher?' But then only the Lord can give the increase and bless his Word (1 Corinthians 3:6–7). Through the difficulties of the church situation, I was shown in a deep way my inability to effect any change and made to feel more dependent on the Lord. In his sovereign wisdom, the Lord had been with his servant, but dealing as much with the preacher and humbling him as with the congregation. Then, again, the ministry of the Holy Spirit cannot be controlled by humans and I learnt afresh that I was unable to turn the tap of blessing on when I wanted. The sovereign, exalted Lord works and gives a greater degree of the Holy Spirit's power in the preaching in his own time and way. He alone convicts of sin and regenerates those of the elect who are spiritually dead and unites them to Christ by faith.

Intense and draining

This period of blessing lasted approximately ten months, but within this brief time-frame young married folk, parents, middle-aged as well as older people were saved, while Christians themselves began to enjoy a deeper intimacy in their relationship with the Lord. There is no space to describe some of the conversions, but the conversion of Barbara Thomas stood out for me. Barbara, a young mother when I started there as pastor, though a church member had stopped attending church services after having her first child. On my several visits to her, she made it clear she would not be returning to church. Accordingly, she was removed from church membership. Six years later, Barbara walked into an evangelistic meeting in the church and was dealt with savingly by the Lord in that meeting, where there was an awesome sense of God's presence. She continued faithfully as a believer until her death and had the joy of seeing her husband, Wyn, trust the Lord before he died.

Some, who were young people at the time, refer to the powerful presence of the Lord in some meetings. At times, the blessing was intense and draining. One missionary, Wolfgang Stumpf, working among Muslims in the Arab world, spoke in the church prayer meeting during this period. At the end of the meeting, he asked me, 'What's happening in this church? Please tell me because the Lord is working here.' I explained briefly the events of previous weeks before Wolfgang left and promised to share more when he returned to the church later in the week. When we next met on the Friday afternoon, Wolfgang shared how he had not slept for two nights after that conversation, but had sought the Lord. Suddenly, in the early hours of the Thursday morning, the Lord had come to him in power, making himself more real to him. Wolfgang's words to me were memorable when we met on the Friday:

> Brother, I understand now why the Lord does not send revival often to his people because we could not stand the intensity of the experience in our mortal bodies. I am exhausted!

And he was right. On reaching my home, he only wanted to lie down on the carpet in front of the coal fire and sleep with the dog next to him! There were also many new opportunities in this period to reach out to unbelievers.

Pub

For a long period, we had felt a burden to reach the hundreds of teenagers and those in their early twenties in the area. It was estimated that, throughout the valley where Maesteg is strategically located, there were well over two thousand youngsters in this age bracket who had lost touch with the churches and the gospel. How could they be reached? As the Lord was graciously at work amongst us, a large public house became available for purchase, located within only a hundred and fifty yards of the church building. The church had no money and the price was prohibitive. Nevertheless, after weeks and weeks of praying, I went to the estate agent's office with a firm assurance to say that I wanted to buy the pub. The agent was interested at first, but then laughed in unbelief when I offered the princely sum of £500 for the large building. He refused to handle the offer as the brewery wanted about £50,000, which in the mid 1960s was a lot of money, especially for a church. The agent, in refusing to convey the offer to the brewery, gave me the address of the brewery for me to contact them. Undaunted, I wrote to the brewery directors, sharing my concern for the plight and needs of the young in the valley and stressing how useful their pub could be for this purpose. Within six weeks I received their response, accepting the offer, but on condition that alcohol was not sold and that they paid legal expenses! Within a few months, the coffee bar was open for the young folk most evenings of the week and they attended in their hundreds over a period of three years. They heard the gospel regularly and there were many excellent gospel conversations and personal Bible studies.

There was a former boxing hall behind the coffee bar which accommodated three hundred people and this was used often on Sunday evenings after church when two to three hundred youngsters would come in for a cold drink and biscuits before hearing the gospel preached. John Thomas, pastor in Sandfields, Aberavon, at the time, came occasionally to preach to these young people, as did others, including Colin Leyshon,[45] who was used on a part-time basis to help with that work. The results? Only the Lord knows. What is known, however, is that all the teens and twenties in the valley heard the gospel, with many prepared to discuss the message. Socially, too, the youngsters had somewhere safe to go in the evenings and relax, which their families appreciated. Good relationships were established with those who came and a few professed conversion as did a small number of parents who have since gone on with the Lord.

Sequel

Within a few months, the denominational church had become a vibrant evangelical church, with many new believers in the fellowship. A period of consolidation and teaching was required, as well as continued outreach. The blessing experienced was, in the Lord's providence and grace, a preparation for future development of the work, which would involve tears, opposition and sacrifice for the church. From late 1968, I was heavily engaged, with the support of others, in leading a theological debate within the English section of the denomination concerning the supreme authority and trustworthiness of the Bible, together with the status of its subordinate standard of faith, the 1823 Confession of Faith. It was a difficult and painful period but that is another story.

The Lord continued to protect his people and a future pastor, the Rev. John Davies, was to witness another movement of the Holy Spirit bringing many young people and some adults to personal faith in Christ during his ministry in Maesteg between 1979 and 1991.

Questions

1. Do you expect God to transform and expand churches today? Explain your answer.

---

45 Colin was a civil servant in Llantrisant at the time and later became minister of Great Stanmore Chapel in North London.

2. Are you familiar with the Bible verses in Luke 11:1–13? Consider the impact these verses had on one pastor as described in this chapter. How do you think the verses are relevant to you and your church?

9. Blessing at the Heath, Cardiff

The Heath Church also had its origins in the Forward Movement of the Presbyterian Church of Wales. Following open-air services and house prayer meetings, a small congregation formed and a hall holding 400 people was built. The church was constituted with eighteen members in January 1901. In the Lord's gracious providence, this small church was richly blessed during the revival of 1904–05 and the Forward Movement appointed a student pastor to lead the work for two years until 1907.

Some miles away in the Rhondda Valley, Trinity Presbyterian Church, Tonypandy, was experiencing considerable blessing during the revival under the ministry of their pastor, Rev. Francis W. Cole. He had begun his ministry there in August 1900 when the church membership stood at 115. By 1905, the membership had increased to 700. In January 1904, a visiting preacher reported

> *a powerful revival has been going on for a number of years now. Many of the worst characters of the district have experienced an evident change ... Last year 163 were received into fellowship from the world ...*

A year later, in January 1905, the local newspaper, *The Rhondda Leader*[46] reported:

> *Last Sunday was a never-to-be-forgotten day in Trinity, Tonypandy. The church is reaping a great harvest of souls ... It is worth recording that for nearly five years hardly a Sunday has passed without a witness of God's saving power in this church ... the church has grown by leaps and bounds ...*

---

46 7 January 1905. See also: D. Geraint Jones, *Revival at Trinity, Tonypandy* (Heath Church Magazine, February/March 2005).

It was Cole, the pastor of this church, who was called to pastor the Heath Church in 1907, where his 'ten years of faithful ministry there bore much fruit as the membership rose from 56 to 517 in 1918.' What is significant is that there has been a succession of godly, evangelical pastors throughout its history. Those immediately preceding Vernon Higham were the Revs. J. Glyn Owen (1948–1954) and W. K. Sharman (1954–1961).

Vernon Higham

Vernon Higham had previously served Welsh language pastorates in Pontarddulais, then Llanddewi Brefi, before being inducted as pastor of the Heath Church in September 1962. The Rev. Dr Gwyn Walters preached in the evening service following the induction. Mr Higham's ministry ended when he retired in 2002. The work was consolidated quickly under Mr Higham's ministry, with an emphasis on the church prayer meeting and outreach in the district, as well as evangelistic preaching meetings in many towns and villages in South Wales. An authorised history of the church reports:

> *It was upon Mr Higham's clear and forthright preaching during the Sunday worship services that God's blessing was most evident … a powerful pulpit ministry was maintained each Sunday, with the morning message being mainly expository and devotional in nature, and the evening having an evangelistic emphasis. The Church's membership, which had remained steady for several years at just over 300, began to increase gradually. Then in February 1965, Mr Higham suffered a severe asthma attack and was dangerously ill in hospital for three weeks. It was feared he might never preach again and, even though he recovered slightly, he required daily medication and frequent hospital treatment.*[47]

Despite his physical weakness, the following years saw the church enjoy a most fruitful period. Mr Higham himself had come into a deep experience

---

47 Leighton Hargest, *Holding Forth the Word of Life: The History of Heath Evangelical Church, Cardiff 1900–2000* (Cardiff: Heath Christian Trust, 2000), pp. 34–35.

of the Lord at this time and there followed a period of remarkable blessing and consolidation between 1965 and the early 1970s, which was marked by large numbers of conversions and the enlivening of believers. Reflecting later on this phase of his ministry, Mr Higham wrote:

> *Meanwhile, without my frenzied efforts and activities, the church … grew — and I virtually stood back and watched it happen. There was no possibility that I could say these were my achievements since all my strength was taken up in keeping alive.*[48]

The church had been stirred to greater prayer for their pastor and his preaching ministry and so additional times of public prayer, as well as smaller prayer groups, were arranged. The pastor often came out of hospital in order to preach, although in considerable physical weakness. It was during this period of illness that he wrote his well-known hymn, which expressed the way the Lord had met with him:

> *I saw a new vision of Jesus,*
> *A view I'd not seen here before,*
> *Beholding in glory so wondrous*
> *With beauty I had to adore.*
> *I stood on the shores of my weakness,*
> *And gazed at the brink of such fear;*
> *'Twas then that I saw Him in newness,*
> *Regarding Him fair and so dear.*
>
> (Christian Hymns, 812)

The opening lines of this hymn are worthy of comment. The phrase 'a new vision of Jesus' refers essentially to biblical statements and truths about the person of Christ with which the author was extremely familiar, but in the hospital ward these verses opened up for him in a profound way. It was as if a brilliant light was focusing on the person of Christ, enabling Mr Higham

---

48 *Holding Forth the Word of Life*, p. 35.

more than ever before to gaze on the Lord's majesty and glory. These were Bible truths he had believed for years, but now he saw the Lord more clearly through the Bible and 'with a beauty' he had to adore. As he 'gazed', the author saw the Saviour 'in newness, regarding Him fair and so dear'. As in many of his other hymns, Mr Higham was able to express in verse his deep, intimate encounters with the Lord, but the cross of the Lord Jesus was always central, as evidenced in *Great is the Gospel of Our Glorious God*.

It is impossible to count the numbers, young and old, locals, students and professionals, who were converted in the Heath Church during the years from 1965 into the 1970s. Prayer continued to be encouraged, numbers in the prayer meetings increased and those converted in that period describe a prayerful sense of expectancy regarding the Sunday preaching services and considerable joy on hearing of people coming to the Lord weekly. Church services were crowded for several years. Mr Higham's illness lasted 'until 1977, by which time the church membership had risen to over 700.'

Impressions and conversions

Ray Russell and his wife were students in Cardiff, studying science in the 1960s, and there were

> *numerous occasions when God's presence was felt as Mr Higham ministered in Heath Church … It was sometimes difficult to sing the final hymn after the sermon, as your heart was in worship to Christ. Hymns such as Immortal Honours Rest on Jesus' Head became especially well-liked in the congregation. Doctrine was alive and the teaching learnt then has served us well for the rest of our lives.*

Wyn Evans describes his impressions when first attending the church as a student in 1967. He was impressed by the number of people present in the Sunday services and the large contingent of students. As an unbeliever, he felt out of place but was impressed by the hymn singing and the pastor's earnest preaching. The welcoming atmosphere also was a factor he remembers well. However, typical of many others, Wyn was not a Christian although he thought he was, due to his Welsh chapel background and the memorising of Bible verses as a child in Sunday School. Arriving in Cardiff as a student in 1965, he started 'living it up' in local pubs, clubs and dance halls but, providentially, he had a girl friend who later informed him she had become a Christian. He joined her in attending the Christian Union and the Heath Church where he '... heard more about the deep love of God ... and how he had sent Christ to die' in the place of sinners like himself. After some struggles, he was converted in April 1967. As a Christian, Wyn became aware of the

> *church increasing in size weekly with new members every communion service. Virtually all of Cardiff University Christian Union attended the church, filling the right-hand side of the church downstairs.*

An informal meeting in the church hall after the evening service

> *was packed each week, mainly of young people. Conversions were virtually on a weekly basis and all considered this to be the norm. It was only when things began to change in the 80s that we realised how much of God's presence we had before ... People were more hungry to learn and grow in the Word. The preaching was powerful and full of meat to feed on and the doctrines were much more clearly included in the preaching then.*

Kerry and Rose Orchard attended the church from October 1974 as unbelievers, but were converted before the end of that year. Kerry writes:

> *The presence of God was tangible. Vernon Higham preached the gospel with great power and there was an expectancy that people would be saved.*

They report that the church 'was fairly full' in the Sunday morning service,

> *but packed in the evening when a 100 or so students came ... also 40 Chinese students (some later formed the Cardiff Chinese*

Christian Church) and some Welsh speakers, who founded the Welsh Evangelical Church in Cardiff.

The church was so packed that the church secretary regularly 'asked people to move along their pews to let latecomers in'!

What about the church prayer meetings? Wyn Evans reports:

Numbers in 1967 were quite low with only about three rows in the middle of the church hall. This grew every week ... I can remember more Scripture being quoted in prayers than now with more emphasis on pleading for revival.

Dave Allan traces his conversion back to 1967 when he had been attending a small Forward Movement cause on the Gabalfa estate, a work which Joyce Akrill (née Dowber) had been leading as a recognised Sister of the People. When she married Richard, she retired from that work and they both entered into membership at the Heath. Dave recalls:

The students from Cardiff Christian Union occupied most of the downstairs seats on the side with not many folk upstairs. There was clear ministry and gospel preaching and an after-meeting every Sunday, which was attended by all ages. Older members talked to us and showed an interest in us. Being invited to tea and then being taken to the evening gospel service by your host was commonplace at that time. Student hospitality was well organised. There would be hymn singing in an after-meeting following the evening service, with refreshments and the pastor or an elder would speak. A testimony would often be given.

The Monday evening Bible Study was well attended as also was the prayer meeting even though the membership was smaller in those days. There was also a Saturday evening meeting for students and young people from the church, held at a church member's home ... it was well attended and very helpful spiritually.

In the early 70s a Saturday morning Bible School was started, with lectures in theology and church history under the auspices of the Evangelical Movement of Wales. The Heath Sunday School was well attended and another Sunday School was started in Lakeside School, which led to some parents and their children coming to Heath Church and for a short while another Sunday School was held on the Llanedeyrn estate.

Dr Martyn Lloyd-Jones visited the church annually to preach mid-week. The meetings were a full house with people from the valleys and neighbouring towns joining us. There was a televised relay set up during the 70s to the hall, but many were disappointed at not gaining entrance to the church. The Word preached was powerful. For me there was a clear moving of the Spirit at this time.

Nigel Counsel refers to personal blessing on the fringe of that more intensive period of blessing. He cannot be more specific than the years 1977 or 1978. He refers to a Sunday evening service in the middle of winter when the church was crowded:

I was sat in the pews in the gallery immediately behind the preacher, Vernon Higham, and he was in the middle of his sermon. Because of the time of the year, many people had coughs and colds so the congregation was rather noisy and restless. Suddenly, I noticed as I looked at the congregation, that everything had become completely still and silent. The only thing that could be heard was Vernon preaching—very powerfully, too. It was as if time was standing still. This lasted for several minutes, though I cannot be sure how long because I was so amazed and affected by the experience.

The second incident took place in a morning service, somewhere around the time of the first. We were singing a hymn—I think it was Immortal Honours. The singing began quite normally, but early in the hymn I suddenly realised that the normal sound of numerous single voices had suddenly become one beautiful single sound like the gentle noise of a flowing river. It was overwhelming. This went on for the rest of the hymn. I had never heard anything like it before, or since. During the preceding years, the Lord had answered prayers and prospered the gospel extensively.

While people were still converted and helped spiritually in the following years until the end of Mr Higham's ministry, the intense period of blessing was confined to the mid-sixties into the early seventies, when weekly conversions were accompanied by the awesome sense of God's presence.

Question

What is your reaction on reading about the Lord's blessing in the Heath Church?

10. Welsh Language Developments

T his chapter considers God's activity in various areas of Wales and in situations that were very different from those described in previous chapters. Nevertheless, the Lord worked powerfully and unexpectedly, albeit briefly, resulting in significant numbers of conversions, especially among young people, while some Christians enjoyed deeper experiences of the Lord.

Aberystwyth

'A landmark event in twentieth-century Welsh language evangelicalism'[49] is how Dr Gwyn Davies described the establishing of a non-denominational Welsh language evangelical church in Aberystwyth. In June 1967, four men—Ieuan Jones, William Morgan, John Ifor Jones and the Rev. Gordon Macdonald—met in Aberystwyth for prayer, seeking the Lord's guidance, for they attended different denominational churches but were concerned because God's Word was not preached faithfully there. They all felt unease, but the decision to leave their denominational churches was made independently by each man. Gordon Macdonald, for example, was a Welsh Wesleyan minister who was convicted he should leave his denomination because of its theological error and unfaithfulness to the gospel of Christ.

The background to this June 1967 meeting is that, in God's providence, a seiat or fellowship meeting was established in the town around November 1964 for local Christians to study the Bible, pray and fellowship together. This seiat met in the home of Dr Bobi Jones and his wife Beti. Dr Bobi had a significant role in leading this regular fellowship meeting but also, as a Welsh language lecturer in the University College of Wales, holding strategic Bible studies and prayer meetings for Welsh students in his college room.

---

49 'A fiftieth birthday in Aberystwyth', *The Evangelical Magazine of Wales*, Nov/Dec 2017, p. 24.

Could a seiat be established in other parts of Wales? That was a desire of the Aberystwyth group, but who would take responsibility for this expansion? In April 1967 Elwyn Davies shared with the seiat that Gordon Macdonald would be resigning from his pastorate outside Aberystwyth in the summer. Contact was made and before long Gordon was leading the seiat in Aberystwyth and had established three more —in Cwmllunau, Caernarfon and Cardigan. The four men in the June 1967 meeting decided to continue to pray about the matter until the Welsh church was opened publicly for worship on the first Sunday of October 1967, meeting in the local YWCA until 1974, with Gordon as its minister. The church has grown and witnessed blessing and conversions and in addition, it has provided a spiritual home for students and locals over the years.

'A bombshell'

Parallel with this development there was blessing amongst the Welsh language university students. Towards the late 1960s, increasing numbers of students were entering the Aberystwyth University College from England, which seriously weakened the Welsh ethos in the Christian Union, making Welsh language students feel uneasy. This was especially critical, as the university had established a Welsh language hall of residence for students by 1968 and there was an urgent need to share the gospel with those students in their language and culture. A small group of Welsh students felt this concern deeply. Gwynn Williams, a ministerial student in the Aberystwyth Theological College, who had studied mathematics in Cambridge, was President of the Christian Union but, with Wyn James and Gwyn Davies, founded the new Welsh language CU, which was for some 'a bombshell'.[50] There was now freedom for specific evangelism amongst Welsh language students and they published several booklets in Welsh. Geraint Fielder reports that

> *Blessing upon their witness to their friends was quite marked, particularly in the early stages ... There were so many conversions*

---

50 *'Excuse me, Mr Davies—Hallelujah!'*, pp. 226–228.

during one academic year that the question 'Who next?' became commonplace amongst Welsh speaking students there. Numbers attending meetings rose from a handful to the fifties at one stage.

This has also been referred to 'as a spiritual awakening'[51] and many of the Welsh students who became Christians found encouragement and fellowship in the newly formed church.

Bangor and North-West Wales

In the 1960s, most places of worship in Bangor and north-west Wales provided services through the Welsh medium. In common with the rest of Wales, Bangor had many chapels and churches but the tide was turning. The blessings of the 1859 and 1904 revivals in Wales were no longer remembered or appreciated, while many churches and chapels were drifting from the truths of the gospel, with congregations dwindling and places of worship beginning to close. The apostolic gospel had ceased to be proclaimed from the pulpits of Bangor, resulting in many a Christian student studying there struggling to find a 'spiritual home' where the gospel was faithfully preached. Local churches and chapels were often liberal or unwelcoming to evangelicals. It was not uncommon for believers from the university's Christian Union to feel spiritually malnourished in Bangor churches; several in the 1960s attended the Gospel Hall in Llanfairfechan, while others travelled as far as Holyhead to Elim and Baptist churches. The work of the CU was hindered by the lack of a clear evangelical church witness in the city.

Providence[52]

In the late 1960s, and unknown to one another at first, two small groups of Christians met independently for Bible study and prayer in Welsh and English. Barry and Maureen Griffith, Betty Williams, Geraint and Elisabeth

---

51 The Evangelical Magazine of Wales, Nov/Dec 2017, p. 25.

52 An official history of the Bangor church is provided in the booklet: Eglwys Efengylaidd EBENEZER Evangelical Church: 50th Anniversary 1969–2019.

Jones and Dewi and Maggie Hughes were among those who met in the Welsh language group. The English language group included Dave Norbury and Hugh Michael. The need for a clear gospel preaching church in the city was felt deeply and by 1969 both groups had discovered one another, agreeing to join together to hold Sunday services in Welsh at 10.00 am and in English at 11.15 am and 6.00 pm. A Welsh Congregational Church building in the city centre, Ebenezer, which dated back to 1805 and had known revivals in its earlier history, became redundant and, with the help of former students and Christians across Wales, the building was purchased and services held there from 17 September 1970. Eryl Davies became the first full-time pastor in October 1975. Attended by many students, both Welsh and English, the urgent need was to develop the church from a preaching station to a local church, then to evangelise the surrounding villages and towns.

Ebenezer encouraged twenty-four of its members and adherents in the establishing in 1980 of the Llangefni Welsh Evangelical Church[53] in Anglesey, under Hywel Davies as pastor. The church also supported the formation of a joint pastorate of two new Welsh language evangelical churches in Talsarnau and Gwyrfai, Gwynedd, under John Glyn, who was ordained in Ebenezer as their pastor in November 1980. While relatively small, all these churches have exercised a significant gospel witness in their localities. In addition, the Rev. Ioan Davies, previously pastoring in Caersalem, Caernarfon, joined the Bangor church to undertake valuable full-time house-to-house visitation in the outlying villages, sharing the gospel. In September 1985, the Bangor Welsh Evangelical Church was formally established by Ebenezer,[54] with the Rev. Dafydd Job as pastor.[55]

There has been blessing and conversions in all these fellowships, but we confine the narrative to a little-known example of blessing in the small church in Gwyrfai.[56]

---

53 Known as Eglwys Cil-dwrn, Llangefni.

54 In addition, a small Welsh Evangelical Church was established in Colwyn Bay in September 1971.

55 Formerly, he was a minister of the Presbyterian Church of Wales. His grandfather was a Calvinistic Methodist Minister in Bethesda at the time of the 1904–5 revival.

56 Now known as Tanycoed, where the Rev. John Pritchard provides valuable ministry.

Gwyrfai[57]

As we have seen, two of the Welsh language evangelical church plants were established in north-west Wales in 1980 under one pastor, John Glyn. The churches were within the Snowdonia National Park but some distance apart, one referred to here as Gwyrfai, near Caernarfon, while the other lay between Porthmadog and Harlech. This is the story of an unexpected degree of blessing over a short period from 1985 in the Gwyrfai church.

The church plant was extremely weak and vulnerable when it was established. The members consisted only of five single young women, although others were in contact with the church. Soon, a family in the village with two children joined the fellowship followed by another family. Nevertheless, the work remained weak, with an average of six to eight, sometimes ten, people attending Sunday services.

In 1982, Dewi Tudor was appointed as an unsalaried assistant pastor to help serve the two churches. Dewi emphasises how weak the church was numerically—they did not know on a weekly basis how many would attend a Sunday service. Part of Dewi's responsibility was to lead the church prayer meeting on Sunday mornings in a nearby village while the pastor preached in Gwyrfai and then on Sunday evenings Dewi would lead the prayer meeting in Gwyrfai while the pastor preached in the other village.

1985

1985 was a significant year for the church. Tom, a local Christian who had been involved in an English-speaking church in the area, joined the fellowship in Gwyrfai. He was a warm Christian. One day, Tom asked Dewi to visit his sister and her husband who lived in Caernarfon, explaining that they were feeling desperate because they were in considerable debt due to business problems. Dewi was welcomed to their home and they shared in detail their problem and the distress they felt. While Dewi tried at times to introduce the gospel into the conversation he failed, but there was a surprise

---

57 I am indebted to the Rev. Dewi Tudor Lewis, pastor of the Welsh Evangelical Church in Talsarnau, for this information which he first shared in the Welsh Pastors' Conference in Bryn-y-groes, Bala.

waiting for him. As he was leaving, they asked whether they could attend his church on the Sunday. Dewi gave them a warm welcome and they arrived for the preaching service. Very soon, they both came to trust in the Lord Jesus Christ. Following their conversion, there was a stream of blessing involving local people with whom they had had no contact at all and would not normally meet socially. About twelve new people came to the Sunday service, seven of whom became Christians while the remaining five attended occasionally.

Shirley

There was another small stream of blessing which encouraged the church. This involved Shirley, who lived nearby in Caernarfon and had been involved with the Jehovah Witnesses, then with the Mormons. She read, or thought she had read, in one of the Mormon booklets the statement that 'even God has a god'. Shirley felt this could not be right, so she checked with local Mormons who affirmed it was what they believed. Shirley was immediately confirmed in her rejection of Mormonism, although months later she could not find the statement in the booklet at all! Before long, Shirley started attending the Gwyrfai church and she too was converted. Shirley was an excellent knitter and one day a woman named Margaret asked her for help in her own knitting; once again the Lord was at work, with Margaret also coming to trust in the Lord Jesus along with one of her close relatives. The church was growing in surprising ways. Within a three-year period from 1985 there was a great change in the church. It was exciting and vibrant and the church felt it was part of something big and important.

Observations

Dewi has made two observations on the blessing in the Gwyrfai church. First, he reminds us that it was the Lord who was responsible for this blessing. Neither he nor the pastor had evangelistic gifts, nor did they hold a mission or have an evangelistic programme. The building where they met was also unattractive, but there was a seriousness amongst the folk. There were no side issues in the preaching, for it majored on the gospel of Christ, with themes like the person of Christ and his sacrifice on the cross for sinners, as well as the need for repentance. Secondly, prayer was emphasised as being essential, but specifically prayer for the work of preaching and church witness. Prayer 'is the work', Dewi reminds us, and church members prayed specifically, not for health or other practical issues, but for the Lord to bless and prosper the preaching of the gospel. There was a burden for the Lord's work amongst them, but also more widely in the land. Dewi asks the question, 'Have we lost sight of the way the Lord is able to break in to our church situations, no matter how difficult?' In the years 1985–1988 there was an unusual degree of blessing on gospel work in which the Gwyrfai church benefited numerically and spiritually.

Questions

1. Was the forming of the Welsh evangelical church in Aberystwyth 'a landmark event'?
2. Are there any observations you want to make on the Bangor story and the church planting in which the church was involved?
3. 'Prayer was emphasised ... specifically prayer for the work of preaching and Christian witness'. What can we learn from this emphasis in Gwyrfai?

11. Clydach, Swansea

The Rev. John Davies (1938–2019) was ordained into the ministry of the Presbyterian Church of Wales in 1964. Initially, he pastored two small Forward Movement churches in the dockland area of Swansea. An outreach work in this needy area had begun under the Forward Movement in 1896 with a mission when there were many conversions. Three years later, a new ministry began, continuing for the next forty-nine years in which the church flourished, despite the poverty and immorality in the area.

By 1964, the church had languished and was in need of new initiatives and pastoral support. John Davies engaged with local people in many ways, but after three years Presbytery asked him to take on two additional churches in the area, one of them being Trinity in the village of Clydach. The church had been keen to obtain his pastoral oversight for it had a history of evangelical ministry under pastors like the Rev. Lewis Evans, who may have been the first evangelical pastor in Trinity. A current member of Bethel Church, Alan Smith, refers to Evans's missionary zeal in the village. E. B. Goronwy was also a pastor in Trinity, with a strong commitment to Christ, which led to his involvement in the annual Keswick in Wales Convention in Llandrindod Wells. D. Leslie Jones succeeded him as pastor, again exercising a solid Bible and pastoral ministry in the church.

During John Davies's ministry, there was increasing disquiet on the part of many evangelical Presbyterian pastors in Wales over the liberal, critical theology which dominated the denomination. The denomination's 1823 Confession of Faith had been thoroughly biblical and God-centred in its theology, but an Act of Parliament in 1933 authorised the re-interpretation of this Confession in the light of modern critical scholarship. This ambiguous re-interpretation was enshrined in a Shorter Confession of Faith, allowing a plethora of interpretations of key doctrines. John Davies eventually informed the elders at Trinity that he was planning to resign from the denomination.

The elders and the church members at Trinity discussed the issue in depth and, following a number of church members' meetings, it was agreed in November 1970 that the church should withdraw from the denomination on 31 March 1971. A 'mini-revival' is how one convert described what the Lord was doing in the church in Clydach under the ministry of John Davies but we need to retrace our steps and provide the context for what the Lord did there in the late 1960s and early 1970s.

Crowded

John Davies tells the story of what happened in the church:

> *During this period of considering secession, the youth meetings in Trinity were crowded. A Christian teacher in the local comprehensive school, Brian Nott, was instrumental in encouraging school pupils to attend the Friday evening youth meetings. These meetings were preceded by prayer sessions when the young and immature Christians prayed for unconverted family and friends.[58] Almost every Friday there would be conversions. In our closing period in Trinity, I referred casually in one service to the fact that there were few men going into theological training.*

Brian Nott and his wife Ann '… were both convinced separately that Brian should respond to God's call to the Christian ministry …' and, after training, Brian served initially as an assistant to Leith Samuel in Above Bar Church, Southampton, and eventually became pastor for many years in Ogmore Vale. Other men from the church were also called to the preaching ministry.

Encouragements

After the church left the denomination in 1971, encouragements in the work continued.

---

58 Mrs Judy Bray (née Minshull) was one of the school pupils taught by Brian Nott and a faithful member of the youth fellowship when John Davies became pastor in Clydach. She confirms the accuracy of what is recorded here.

We were still meeting in a temporary building, the Red Cross Hall in Clydach. One Sunday morning, in the middle of the service, in trooped three hippies! One was Nigel Clifford who had earlier come under conviction, and had sought out a former workmate who advised him to come to us. His testimony is another story. He had been involved in drug dealing and was well-known to the Swansea Police Drug Squad. Nigel became very involved with us, and later was called into the ministry ... and also one of our young people, Andrew Bowden, felt called into the Christian ministry and he married one of our young people, Gwyneth Rees. By this time, we had bought a vacant Church in Wales building[59] in the village ... Church members set to in renovating the interior and Bethel became our home!

John and his family moved into temporary accommodation in a local council flat and met several young families like their own. John's wife, Joan, started a Bible study in their home for women in their block of flats and among those attending was Lyn, a mother of three, who was soon converted and started attending Bethel with her children. Lyn's husband Keith 'was not interested in the gospel but was involved in witchcraft, and styled himself a white witch. He was not aggressive towards me or the gospel, but was not interested.' One day he sought the pastor's help—he had obeyed a 'spirit' and did so by hitting his wife repeatedly in the night. He realised that this was wrong. John introduced him to a colleague, but then did not see him for a period afterwards 'until a chance meeting in Neath when he invited me into his house. By this time, he was separated from his wife Lyn. In our meeting, he agreed to attend church. He was later converted.'

Another conversion related to an elderly neighbour of a church member, Wil Thomas, who had started attending church.

---

59 Alan Evans, an elder of the church, is of the opinion that this was the first time for the Church in Wales to sell one of their redundant church buildings to a Nonconformist church. He suggests one reason was that the local vicar at the time was sympathetic towards the work there.

He did not have a good name in the village. He had been a troublesome neighbour and there were other stories about him too. He was a widower and had lost many of his fingers in the saw machine so as to avoid going into the army! He was converted in his late 60s. In one memorable prayer meeting, Wil Thomas had confessed how rotten a sinner he was—the worst of all. Then afterwards Wil Jones got up and prayed, saying, 'Lord, don't listen to Wil Thomas, I am the worst sinner of all!'

Both men were characters, but with a deep sense of sin and appreciation of the Lord's grace in saving them.

Blessing and growth

How long did the period of blessing last? 'It's difficult to assess the period of blessing,' John replied.

Prior to leaving the denomination we were already experiencing blessing and growth. In our prayer meetings there was certainly a cry coming from the hearts of both young and old. When we moved into the Red Cross Hall in April 1971, there was a buzz in the church. It's impossible to record all the blessings without the danger of overstating events. But let me refer to two more conversions at this time.

We always had a service on New Year's evening. The majority of the congregation were young people who spent the evening in our home. We would all walk from the house to the service at Bethel for 11.30 pm. Colin and Jean Wooldridge always came to collect their three children, and one year decided to attend the service. Later that week Colin told me of God's dealings with him in that service which led to his conversion. His wife was converted soon afterwards. They still attend Bethel with a daughter and their other daughters are also going on with the Lord.

Opposed

Then there was the conversion of a church member's husband, who was very opposed to the gospel and the church. He had worked as a baker and suffered from lung problems. He was an unpleasant man and always left the room when I visited their home. Later he was admitted into Morriston hospital and in visiting him I was unsure how he would receive me. I sat with him and we talked freely but when it was time to leave him, I felt unsure whether to read from the Bible and pray with him. I stood up ready to leave when he gripped my arm and said, 'Aren't you going to pray?' I did so and left, but there were further conversations. On a second period in hospital, I called to see him and he wanted to hear about the gospel. I readily explained the gospel to him. On his arrival at the bedside, the son ordered me to leave, but his father insisted I had to stay because I had told him what he needed to know. Amazingly, he came to personal faith in the Lord Jesus Christ. A short time later, I was called to the hospital and prayed with him before he entered glory.

Impact

I asked John concerning the impact this period of blessing had on the church and on him personally. What place did prayer have in his own life? He replied:

In the early 1970s I was already concerned about gospel witness in Wales. I had started attending, with other pastors like Elwyn Davies, Luther and Neville Rees, a Friday morning prayer meeting for revival. We met in the mission in Cwmtwrch. Pastor George Griffiths, converted in the 1904 revival, led the meeting. He was a godly man and longed for the Holy Spirit to move in Wales again in power. It was a challenge to me and to others present.

The background to this prayer meeting is interesting. George Griffiths (1885–1970) had been used to establish the Cwmtwrch Mission Hall, known as Tro'r Gleien Mission Hall, which he pastored for decades. In the early 1960s, two pastors in the Swansea area, Luther Rees and I. B. Davies, found great encouragement and support in fellowshipping with Griffiths. Gradually, and stirred by the possibilities held out to them, a few younger men sought to initiate a movement of prayer, under Griffiths' leadership, with the sole aim of saying to God, 'O Lord, do it again'. Young pastors regularly wanted to visit and learn about revival from him, but he was concerned about this and began to urge them to pray, instead of merely listening to him recounting the Lord's work in revival. Beginning in 1968, these prayer meetings were held every Friday morning and continued weekly until 1982. From 1982, the prayer meeting took on the form of special 'days of prayer' and then 'half-days of prayer', held quarterly in Bridgend, initially under the leadership of Elwyn Davies. Following the 1981 Bala Pastors' Conference, pastors agreed to pray for one another each Saturday evening and for the Lord's blessing on the preaching of the gospel, with some pastors also meeting with their church elders to seek God for revival.

John Davies refers to a more personal experience of the Lord:

An even more powerful experience of the Lord occurred when I was admitted into Singleton Hospital in Swansea during the August Bank holiday in 1974 with a suspected deep vein thrombosis. While reading my Bible, I was in considerable pain so the night nurse sent for the duty doctor and the following is an extract I wrote in my Thompson Bible the following day:

'Whilst in hospital the Lord was pleased to draw near to me in a wonderful way. It was a little of heaven on earth. I became unaware of pain, although I was in great pain, and my heart was drawn out in love and adoration to him who loved me and died for me. I was reading 2 Timothy chapter 1 at the time, especially verses 9 and 10, and those verses caused me to praise him because he confirmed to me powerfully the great salvation I was a partaker of and the great gospel I was to preach … that I may know him (Philippians 3:10).'

Chapter 11

The Lord did something special in our lives. I said nothing about this to the church elders but when I eventually returned to the pulpit to preach, one of the elders asked me after preaching, 'What's happened to you?'

John explained that

having known this recent encounter with the Lord—I don't know how to describe it—I cannot be content with anything less.

He added:

Although we were knowing blessings in the church, we were not unique, for the Lord was moving in other parts of Wales and the UK. But I want to relate another example of the Lord's working at this time in 1976.

Each summer, my wife Joan and I took a group of our young people to Llanymawddwy, near Bala. We rented the old farm house belonging to John and Mari Jones, which was a working sheep farm. In 1976 we took over twenty-five of our young people there. It wasn't possible to accommodate them all in the house, so we had tents in the grounds as well. Joan did the cooking, with the youngsters contributing their various skills in preparation and washing dishes. The programme was set around a daily morning Bible study, which I led. The afternoons were free, with visits to Bala and the beach, and also walks in the hills. The evenings were devoted to prayer and discussion. The theme this particular year was from Isaiah 6. One of the new songs we were singing was Holy, Holy, Lord God Almighty. As the days passed, this song was being sung at every opportunity— on the mini-bus, in the house, outside, and even on the beach. It was clear the Lord was working amongst us. As the week progressed it became a time of brokenness, and also conversions. Among others, our daughter Helen, a nine-year-old, professed faith. There was a sense of the awesome presence of God and I had not known anything like it before. The Friday night was devoted to prayer, and what a prayer meeting! Some young people were in tears. One of the young men rushed outside. My wife followed him, and in tears he kept saying 'God is inside of me'. It was the early hours of the morning before I was able to close the meeting and, even then, some were reluctant to go. I wrote the following in the front of my Thompson Bible the following week:

'August 13th, 1976. Llanymawddwy YPF. The evening prayer meeting. The Lord came down, the Holy Spirit caused us to praise and exalt him. The prayer time continued for hours. An unforgettable and glorious experience. The same night our own Helen (nearly 9 years old) brought to the Lord. Praise Him. Ephesians 5:18.'

It was a taste of revival and the Lord heard our cry and this blessing continued not only with the youth but also with older people in the church.

'Mini-revival'?

Was this period really a 'mini-revival'? Pearl Hentzschel claims it was, as did some of her peers. Brought up in Clydach and attending this family-orientated church, she spent much time, along with others, with the pastor and his wife, as well as Sunday School teachers. She writes:

The church was wonderfully kind and generous to us as youngsters … guiding us to seek the Lord Jesus … We felt cherished and loved within the church fellowship … People in the church provided spiritually and morally excellent role models to us as youngsters … Many young people were becoming influenced by the huge drug culture at that time … The alternative life style we were being shown … was a breath of fresh air…

Attending Scripture Union in school at lunch times twice a week, with thirty to forty pupils present was *memorable, while our church was thriving with more and more people of all ages beginning to attend. To all intents, there was a kind of mini-revival beginning to happen amongst the local people and youth of Clydach.*

Pearl herself was eventually converted in a Bible rally and 'felt as though my heart was bursting with new happiness' and she shared what had happened with John Davies, her pastor. 'To my complete surprise', Pearl adds,

I was not aware that at least two other young people had also been converted during the rally … During the following months the mini-revival was in full swing in the church, going from strength to strength, until it reached its peak with at least thirty more young people and also some older people coming to know Christ, some of whom had led very troubled lives, many having been once heavily involved in drugs.

Only a few months before he died in November 2019, John Davies concluded with these memorable words:

As I reflect on those times and the blessings we experienced and the awesome awareness of God which was so real then, I cannot be content with anything less today.

Questions

1. What are your main impressions after reading this chapter?
2. Would you describe events in the church at Clydach as a 'mini-revival'? Explain your answer.
3. 'My heart was drawn out in love and adoration to him who loved me and died for me.' Is this a reality we are familiar with, or seeking, in our lives?

12. Merthyr Tydfil

Park Baptist Chapel in Merthyr is an evangelical church. In the 1950s and 1960s the members were mostly Arminian in doctrine but with a smaller, significant number of believers committed to Calvinism, emphasising the sovereignty of God in creation, providence and salvation. The gospel had been preached regularly in Park for years and while we will focus on a brief report of blessing in the church by Lindsay Brown,[60] I would emphasise that there were conversions over the years in the church. Pastor Iorwerth Budge served there faithfully for a period of forty years.

One example of someone being converted in the early 1960s is that of Owen Jones, who was brought up in Merthyr Tydfil and, as a child sent to Sunday School. He left school at the age of fifteen in order to start work in a local factory, where he helped in making prams and pushchairs. He had no knowledge of God and was not interested in Christianity, but rather followed the cultural norm of drinking to excess and, as a consequence, he fell deeper into sin. God in his sovereign providence and grace brought a man to work near him when he was employed at the local Hoover factory, Pentrebach, where they made washing machines. This man told Owen that he had been converted twenty-five years earlier and he wanted to take Owen to a church service at Park Chapel. Owen agreed to go with him and in Park on Sunday, 8 September 1963, he asked the Lord Jesus Christ to come into his life and save him. Owen began a new life and became an entirely new person. At the same time, a fresh view was given him of what he could do for the Lord Jesus as a nineteen-year-old man.

A gifted preacher, Hywel Griffiths of Litchard Mission, Bridgend, came to Park Chapel one Sunday morning. His text was from 1 Chronicles 4:10: "'Oh, that you would bless me indeed, and enlarge my territory, that your hand would

---

60 Email correspondence, 23/01/2020.

be with me, and that you would keep me from evil, that I may not cause pain." So God granted him what he requested.' About that time the London City Mission (LCM) was inviting young men to a conference at Felixstowe to learn about the possibility of serving the Lord in the city of London. Owen applied to LCM and four years later he and his wife moved to West Norwood where they worked for six years in Bethel Mission and in Lothian Road, Brixton. Later, Owen pastored a church in the south of England. He remarks that when he moved to London, 'The Lord was doing a significant work among teenagers on a Friday night at Park Chapel, Merthyr Tydfil, with lasting effects.'

Lindsay Brown, who was converted in 1967 at the age of thirteen, takes up the story. 'The person who shaped me most was my maternal grandmother', he writes. Due to his grandfather dying when he was seven years old, Lindsay's parents sent him to stay with his grandmother briefly, but that stay lasted for twelve years although he saw his parents daily. His grandmother was God-fearing, and sent him to Sunday School where he was eventually converted. Raymond Powell, a railwayman, was the church secretary and Sunday School superintendent at Park Chapel and, as soon as Lindsay was converted, he encouraged him to speak in open-air meetings, then made him a Sunday School teacher at the age of fourteen. Ray had a great influence on Lindsay's life. Lindsay continues the story:

> *At that time, there was a youth group of only around fifteen in the church. Soon after I was converted, I started a Christian Union in Merthyr County Grammar School, which I attended. In June/July 1970, a group of us went to Cardiff to hear Arthur Blessitt speak, a well-known American evangelist who went around carrying a cross. God touched us that day and we asked Pastor Budge if we could take the Sunday service the following week, to share what we'd heard. Unknown to us, that same weekend another boy (Kevin Williams) from the youth group had been at Filey Bible Week and God had similarly spoken to him. As a result of the fresh impetus of these meetings, we decided on a three-fold course of action.*

First, we started two early morning prayer meetings before school at 7.00 am every Wednesday and Saturday, praying for the town. Secondly, it was a time of transition from the grammar to the comprehensive education system, and a group of us moved to form a large sixth form at Cyfarthfa Castle Comprehensive, where we started Christian Unions for three age groups, namely, those under 13, those 13–16 years old, then also the whole school. Through these CUs many pupils were converted, especially during one period of six months when we experienced students professing faith every day! That was exciting. Thirdly, we also started open-air meetings in Merthyr town every Saturday. As a result of these efforts, the church youth group grew from 15 to between 220–250 in one year, with many young people converted principally through the CUs and the youth group at Park Baptist Chapel. During this time, we were joined by the youth group at Elim Church, Dowlais; we often met in Park on a Friday evening and at Elim on Saturday evenings and called the youth group 'Baptecostal' youth group! Quite a number of them married within this group; some drifted away later on, but many stood firm and went on to serve the Lord for many years afterwards.

This growth lasted for about 3 years, till most of the key leaders had left for university. I subsequently saw a number of these young people in leadership positions in CUs across Wales when I was a UCCF staff-worker from 1977–1981. About five young men became pastors, in Swansea, Mumbles, Aberdare, Harpenden and elsewhere in England, and several became long-term missionaries, including myself with IFES and Gaynor Pritchard (née Powell), who was involved in leadership of a mission agency called People International, an agency seeking to reach out to people in central Asia. Gaynor had been youth leader before me and had encouraged the young people to be involved in fasting over a Friday lunchtime and then giving the money saved toward supporting the persecuted church in Eastern Europe.

At the Evangelical Movement of Wales Annual English Conference in Aberystwyth in August 2019, Lindsay reported that he met there as many as fifteen former members of the youth group in Park Church who

> *also have had significant roles in their professional lives as teachers, head teachers and medical doctors and they are still pressing on, over forty-five years after they were converted! Quite a number of those young people became Sunday School teachers, deacons, elders and held other leadership positions in churches, both in Wales and beyond.[61] It was a remarkable period of growth. I do believe that God was in it and, having seen God at work at that time, it gave many of us great confidence that God can work similarly later on in life. It was a special experience for which we thank God.*

Major factors in the growth

Although Iorwerth Budge served as pastor in Park Church for forty years, Lindsay suggests that

> *the major factors, under God, in the church's growth were neither the new Charismatic Movement of the mid/late 1960s, nor the powerful preaching of Dr D. Martyn Lloyd-Jones in alternate years until the early 1970s, nor the Evangelical Movement of Wales.*

He identifies four major factors. First,

---

61 Lindsay himself studied European history in Oxford and became President of the Christian Union. He has been involved in student ministry in Wales with UCCF 1978–1981 and with the International Fellowship of Evangelical Students (IFES) from 1981, serving as General Secretary from 1991–2007. He was seconded part time to the Lausanne Movement from 2008 and spends the rest of his time with the IFES–FEUER (Fellowship of Evangelists in the Universities of Europe) network which seeks to stimulate the public communication of the gospel in universities across Europe. He is convinced of the strategic importance of student work for the continuing health and strength of the worldwide church. It was at university that he developed his foundational convictions, including a strong commitment to the importance of Scripture and expository preaching and the recognition that personal testimony, specific prayer, and clear presentation of the gospel formed a powerful and effective combination in evangelism. Lindsay also served as the International Director for the Lausanne Movement and is the author of *Shining like Stars*—a collection of student stories from the 20th century.

godly lay people like Ray Powell. He was a very godly man and for most of the period of 40 years when Pastor Budge ministered in the church, Ray Powell[62] *was the church secretary. Many of the key youth leaders in the church (including myself, Gaynor, and my successor, Kevin Williams, who is currently church secretary) became believers on the Galon Uchaf housing estate, adjacent to the famous Gurnos estate. Ray worked on the railway and he was a humble layman who had a global influence through the people converted under his influence This man was a key to the steady growth of the church in Park.*

Secondly, 'the three Sunday Schools set up by Mr Powell and Rev. Budge who were good friends and worked closely together. These Sunday Schools were blessed by the Lord.' Thirdly, 'the school CUs and youth group were major factors where blessing was experienced'. Finally, Lindsay refers to the so-called 'Jesus Movement' of the late 60s, which started in California and came to the UK through people like Arthur Blessitt, the evangelist. Although unconventional, he believes this evangelist had 'a deep love for the Lord and a passion to reach unbelievers with the gospel'.

Questions

1. In what ways can Christian teenagers take initiatives for the gospel?
2. Reflect on the prayer meetings held. Are there any aspects which challenge and encourage you?
3. How does Ray Powell's life and influence challenge you?

---

62 The father of Gaynor Pritchard (née Powell).

13. Gospel Progress in Llamsamlet

Luther Rees

The Rev. Luther Rees (1908–1982)[63] had been orphaned at the age of fourteen and went to live with an aunt and her family who moved to New Road, Skewen, where the father, a master baker, obtained bakery premises. Providentially, although the family moved back to Cardiff on retirement, Luther remained in Skewen for he had met his wife there and married in April 1933. Converted to Christ while reading Psalm 103, he attended the Free Mission Church, Dynevor Road, Skewen until 1949, when he became a lay pastor and remained there until 1953. It was in June 1953 that Luther suffered a physical breakdown, but in this strategic period his only son Neville was converted and he himself also felt a deep sense of call to be a preacher of the gospel. For the purpose of ministerial training, Luther entered the Memorial Theological College in Brecon in September 1954 and studied until 1957. His longing was for people to receive and love the Lord Jesus Christ. While serving as a lay pastor in Skewen Mission on Sundays, he had seen grieving people coming in saving faith to the Lord Jesus and the small congregation of about forty grew to over one hundred and fifty with regular conversions.

Peniel Green, Llansamlet

In July 1957, Luther Rees was inducted as the full-time pastor of Peniel Green Congregational Church in Llansamlet, Swansea but the church at the time was very different from what he had known in Skewen Mission. It was liberal in its theology and many members were strangers to God's grace in Christ. Opposition was inevitable and the church prayer meetings

---

63 My sincere thanks to the Rev. Neville Rees for this information and also to Lucy Beale for details of her testimony.

were difficult. Luther was a mature man with a great love for the people and gradually a number of them began to respond to the preaching of the gospel. One of the converts was Idwal Richards, who taught woodwork in a local school before he became the headmaster of the Junior Comprehensive School in Llansamlet. The Lord was at work, for his entire family came to personal faith in Christ. The deacons, as well as members, were challenged by Luther's preaching and pastoral work. The senior deacon was responsible for leading the hymn singing in the Sunday church services. One evening, he broke down in a church prayer meeting and was wonderfully broken in repentance and faith. He became a different person in Christ. Slowly the church began to change and the 1960s and early 1970s were significant periods in terms of blessing and gospel progress. Whole weeks of gospel preaching had been introduced periodically, with local pastors like Emrys Davies, Swansea, evangelist Idris Davies, Ammanford, I. B. Davies, Neath, and Elwyn Davies, General Secretary of the Evangelical Movement of Wales, invited to preach the gospel and their preaching was greatly appreciated.

Testimony

Lucy Beale was converted in the church in 1963. She had attended Sunday School from an early age and went to the morning church service on her own. Luther Rees became her Sunday School teacher. Lucy enjoyed these classes and started attending the Friday youth meeting. But it was in a week of mission in Peniel Green that Lucy says she was converted. On 24 November, Elwyn Davies preached from John 14:6 on the words, 'I am the way, the truth and the life ...' Lucy takes up the story: 'I knew I was at a cross roads.' Later that evening, after speaking with the pastor, she trusted in the Lord Jesus. 'I told all my friends that I had been converted. Eventually all six of my Glanmor School friends came to trust in the Lord Jesus and three of us married ministers.'

What were her outstanding memories of the church at this time?

> *Everyone who was converted came to the weekly prayer meeting at Peniel Green and there were so many wanting to pray that it*

was difficult to get a word in. It was a wonderful meeting ... I am
so thankful for my home church, Peniel Green. Eventually I was
to meet my future husband, Rev. Alan Tovey there, while he was
staying with the Rev. and Mrs Luther Rees, and we married in 1974.

Luther Rees remained as pastor at Peniel Green until 1977, completing
twenty years of ministry in the fellowship. His immediate successor weakened
the work of the church so it was a joy for the church later to welcome Brian
Higham as its pastor.

Brian Higham

The church invited Brian Higham, a teacher, to become its pastor and he
began his ministry in September 1979, with a combined ordination and
induction service in November when Lloyd-Jones was the guest preacher.
One member, Terry Norris, 'was saved in that service while Dr Lloyd-Jones
was preaching. At the time, Lloyd-Jones felt that it was a seal on the work
here.'[64]

Writing nine months later, the new pastor reported that

before long there seemed to be a new spirit in the church and during
the ensuing months the members were themselves encouraged to
see new faces appearing steadily in the congregation. Perhaps the
most hopeful sign of all was that the prayer meeting began to see a
steady increase.

He affirmed that despite 'practical difficulties it is a joy to see that there is
a sense of awareness of God Almighty working amongst us and that he is a
God who answers prayers.'[65]

After Brian Higham had pastored the church for nearly two years, we are
informed 'that there has been quite a noticeable change' with 'a new core of

---

64 Heath Church Magazine, February–March, 2007, p.10: Max Munday, *A Touch of Heaven in*
Llansamlet.
65 Heath Evangelical Church Newsletter, No.4, July/August 1980, p.6.

faithful believers ... in effect, we have a new church ... growing in our midst.' The number attending morning services increased significantly, but

we have been encouraged in the most important area of church life—that of the prayer meeting. The attendance has grown steadily and about a third that attend are young people recently converted.[66]

Several months later, Brian Higham's report is even more encouraging as 'so much has happened.' He refers to a Sunday during the winter

when South Wales was hit by the blizzard and God also began to reveal himself in a new way to many of us ... From that time onwards our prayers for conversions were answered in a remarkable way and some key people in the fellowship were also blessed. Since those bleak winter days, God has smiled constantly upon us, the prayer meeting has steadily increased ... and the urgency has increased as well in the praying. The congregations these last few weeks have shown a marked increase ... Backsliders have returned and known once more the blessedness they knew when first they saw the Lord...[67]

A year later we learn that the church

continues to see the hand of God upon it ... we have been aware of a deepening in the spiritual lives of many of the people ... These last few weeks we have also been aware of the Lord working in the lives of the youth of the church...[68]

The pastor's report early in 1984 refers to him having been pastor there for four years but, alongside church growth, he acknowledges 'problems', with the last few months having 'been very difficult'. Nevertheless, there were encouragements regarding the number of children in Sunday School and 'the

---

66 Heath Evangelical Church Newsletter, No. 4, July/August 1981, p. 10.
67 Heath Evangelical Church Magazine, No. 3, May/June 1982, pp. 7–8.
68 Heath Evangelical Church Magazine, No. 2, March/April 1983, p. 12.

crowds of children' in the Friday Club. He also reported that 'attendance at prayer meeting is very encouraging.'[69]

Professor Max Munday was converted in the church in 1984, and was one of the later converts in the early years of Brian Higham's ministry. He regards the period of blessing as beginning in 1980 and continuing over a period of approximately six years when 'God did a work here.' However, he emphasises that Peniel Green was not the only church in the area that experienced blessing and growth during these years. Past blessing and growth in Peniel Green meant that in 1979 there were faithful deacons and church members, although the church congregation was becoming elderly. What had impressed Max when arriving from Lancaster in 1984? His answer is:

> *There was a real brightness, sharpness and a light about the people. There was a measure of happiness and contentment that you see in newly converted people … A lot of people of different ages had been converted and that light was shining out of them … There was a new light shining there …*

What else did he notice?

> *I saw a cleanness and a great spirit of community … People gossiped the gospel either in their daily work or with neighbours … I saw people helping one another … there was a much greater urgency in the prayer meeting. A lot more of us prayed. There were a lot more tears … So many people wanted to pray … a far greater sense of anticipation. People were mentioned and you saw them being saved. Very blessed also at this time were the Bible studies … There was a hunger for the Word of God … You had a hungry people who wanted to move from the milk to the meat of the Word.*

Were there further aspects which impressed Max?

---

69 Heath Evangelical Church Magazine, Issue Number 2, March/April 1984, p. 10.

There were some surprising and extraordinary conversions. People you thought would never be saved were wrought upon by the Spirit of God ... Backsliders restored, after ten, fifteen or twenty years previously making a profession, and returned to God ... there was forgiveness

following a split.[70]

Questions

1. Can you identify any important principles and changes in the Llansamlet church situation?
2. Are there aspects of church life from 1979 onwards you want to draw attention to?

---

70 Heath Church Magazine, February–March, 2007, 'A Touch of Heaven in Llansamlet', Max Mundy, p. 112.

14. Abergavenny: Strategic Ministries

Whitefield Presbyterian Church in Pen-y-pound, Abergavenny, celebrated its centenary in 1971. For the occasion, the minister, the Rev. Geraint Fielder, wrote a brief history of the church,[71] tracing its links before 1871 to 1818, 1744, 1739, 1646, and even as far back as the late fourteenth century, for some '... members of the church in 1971 were collateral descendants of Walter Brute, one of the greatest of the Lollards'. The Lollards were followers of John Wycliffe (d.1384) who 'prepared the way for the Protestant Reformation in the sixteenth century by preaching the gospel and providing the Scriptures in the language of the people'. One of those Lollards, Walter Brute, was an Oxford graduate, born near Abergavenny.

His preaching in the area (in Welsh) and his influential writings made the Welsh Marches one of the most important spheres of Lollard influence outside Oxford itself. The scriptural faithfulness of Brute's views was extraordinary for his times, and he anticipated, by more than a century, the teachings of Martin Luther. Descendants of Brute's family formerly worshipped at our church at Forest Coalpit. From there some moved to Ebbw Vale and Abergavenny. The members with us (in 1971) took the name Bruten early this century.

Many well-known preachers and Christian leaders had links with Abergavenny. 'Richards Symonds and Walter Cradock were both significant Nonconformist pioneers', both converted under the preaching of William Wroth of Llanvaches. Symonds, an Oxford graduate, was born in Abergavenny and was the first 'Presbyterian' preacher from this town. In 1646 he was approved by the Westminster Assembly of Divines to be an itinerant minister of the gospel in Wales.

---

71 Geraint D. Fielder, *Whitefield's Presbyterian Church, Abergavenny, 1871–1971.*

In the eighteenth-century, Howel Harris often stayed in Abergavenny and

worked closely with George Whitefield from the earliest years of the Revival, with Abergavenny chosen occasionally as a meeting point for them. Whitefield preached here first on the 5th April 1739 and reports:' God impressed a divine awe upon all, so that though there were many opposers present when I preached, yet not one dared to utter a word ... God caused me to speak with extraordinary authority. Oh, that they might come to the knowledge of the truth and be saved'. Wesley paid his first visit here on 15th September 1739. He preached twice, in the same garden as Whitefield, to upwards of 1,600 people.

A Calvinistic Methodist society, or fellowship, had by now been founded in Abergavenny by Howel Harris, probably sometime between 1739 and 1741.

'Remarkable heritage!'

Geraint Fielder, with some delight, emphasised:

Here is the source of our own church. What a remarkable heritage! The work was started through the ministry of three of the most powerful advocates of the gospel that God has raised up in this or any land.

However, he added:

We know very little of the subsequent history of the society/fellowship but we do have some details of the marriage of one of its leading local supporters—Elizabeth James—to George Whitefield in 1741, whose name was to be given to the church that was erected in 1871. In 1744 Whitefield was again back in the town this time as Moderator of a joint English and Welsh Association of Calvinistic Methodists.
Some 'Presbyterians' were still found in the town and area in later years, including a Calvinistic Methodist pastor in the Congregational

Church (1818–1831). Later, in 1868, the Welsh Presbyterian pastor in Crickhowell began to preach to a nucleus of Christians in Abergavenny, which resulted in the formation of Whitefield Church in 1871 with ten members. Growth was slow, with many challenges facing the young church.

Highlights

Highlights in subsequent years included the Annual Report for 1895 which read, 'The Lord has been in the midst of the church indeed', especially 'the real increase of the church from the world by conversion rather than by transfer from other churches'. The Annual English Conference of the denomination was held in the church from 19th–21st September 1899. These early conferences were rich in biblical exposition, in intellectual debate and in attempts to grapple with current affairs. Sadly, the debates revealed that 'there were some leaders who were having serious doubts about the truths of our faith. There was also rumour of unbelief among church members. Our own minister, W. S. Jones, had spoken out on this in the 1894 Conference at City Road, Chester. He had heard it asserted that many members within our churches were virtually Unitarians, if not materialists. W. S. Jones held that he could not believe in the "salvation of any man who does not accept the Deity of Christ."' The 1904–05 revival affected the surrounding area although not directly Whitefield Presbyterian Church.

In 1912, John Millward, succeeded to the pastorate … His 12 years of ministry here were times of real spiritual advance. His comments in the church manual for 1916 show the priorities of his ministry. The church had just had a Ten-Day Mission. 'For a long time, the Church of God has been feeling that something is wrong. We have been so powerless in the face of sin, even though our gospel is the power of God; we have witnessed such ease in Zion that we have become ashamed of our profession of Christ.' 'What has been the matter with us? What has been wrong? Have we not believed? Have we not received Christ? Are we not His? Yes; yes; still, something is amiss! We have been uncharitable, jealous, self-centred. We have not presented ourselves as a living sacrifice.' The Mission was 'not only a "Call to the Unconverted" but also an exhortation to believers to enter into the fullness of their inheritance in the Holy Spirit.' 'A great blessing to the church', reported the elders on this mission. The senior elder at this time—Mr Sam Davies, senior ... had been deeply blessed of God in the 1859 Revival. 'I loved to hear him speak on the great doctrines of grace and I loved equally to hear him pray, with the dew of Heaven upon him', said Mr Millward.

Failing momentum

When Millward left in 1924, the membership had risen to 176, but there were also signs of failing momentum. The Great War had left its mark; the mood of the times was extremely frivolous. The prayer meeting had fewer people attending and the Sunday morning congregation was becoming a cause for concern. The church was also a 'fashionable' church. When the Rev. Howell Williams, arrived in 1940 as minister of the church, the prayer meeting had temporarily lapsed and the congregations were at their lowest for many a year, with membership down to 128. Despite having two further ministers, the spiritual and numerical decline of the church continued with no weeknight services being held at all during 1965.

W. K. Sharman

It is important to refer to the brief ministry of the Rev. W. K. Sharman which, though it lasted in Abergavenny for only twenty months from 1966, was strategic in several ways, especially in preparing the way for Geraint Fielder's ministry. Originally from Neath, 'Jack' Sharman was converted in the Forward Movement Mission Hall, Neath, in 1928, while his wife Pegi became a Christian in Sandfields, Aberavon, under the preaching of Lloyd-Jones who was the pastor at the time. Pegi wrote, 'What had hitherto been theoretical became actual in my experience and in Christ my soul found safety and satisfaction.'[72] Pegi, with a strong sense of call to China, undertook two years of training in London and sailed on 11 September 1936 with twelve other women for mission work in China. Jack had earlier followed the same training course and had sailed for China on 20 September 1934. Both Jack and Pegi were well aware of the dangers, as the civil war was raging, nevertheless they felt called to share the gospel of Christ in that country.

Jack had met Pegi over a meal before going to China, but she 'was blissfully ignorant of his feelings' for her. Having prayed for two years that the Lord would allow them to meet, Jack wrote to Pegi before she finished language school in China to arrange a meeting. The rest is history; they married in Shanghai in 1938, serving in China until 1950 when they were amongst the last missionaries compelled to leave the country as the persecution of believers gathered momentum. Back in the United Kingdom, Jack Sharman was ordained into the ministry of the Presbyterian Church of Wales, assuming responsibilities for two Forward Movement churches in Cardiff, which included Saltmead. Later, from 1954–1961 he became pastor of Heath Presbyterian Church, Cardiff, and witnessed significant blessing, 'particularly evident in the work amongst young people'[73] and students with some being called to missionary work overseas. Ceri Douglass, Sharman's daughter, adds that her father

> *had a very fruitful ministry in Cardiff ... He saw a wonderful opportunity of reaching people influential in their own countries with the love of Christ, so he visited each overseas student who came to Cardiff with a welcome gift of an English Bible and an invitation to his church. Many overseas students came to know Christ during their time in Cardiff and went back to their own countries able to share their new found faith in the risen Christ.*[74]

---

72 China Memoirs of Jack & Pegi Sharman, compiled by Ceri Douglass, ii.
73 Holding Forth the Word of Life: The History of Heath Evangelical Church, Cardiff 1900–2000, pp. 28–30.
74 China Memoirs of Jack & Pegi Sharman, Postscript, p. 4.

By 1961, the Sharmans felt they should join the staff of the Overseas Missionary Fellowship (formerly CIM) at their head office in London.

By late 1965, Jack Sharman knew it was time to return to Wales as a Presbyterian pastor. Ceri Douglass provides the background for us:

> *I was surprised when I was told that Dad was going to become the pastor of a church that was thinking of dropping the evening service because they couldn't afford to heat the church and it was also fairly liberal in its teaching. He specifically asked the Presbytery for a struggling church. I imagined that having previously been the minister of a large church in Heath, that Dad would have gone to a similar sized church. I was in my teens at the time and remember him telling me that God's ways are different from the ways of the world that tends to climb ladders of success but Jesus left heaven to come to earth and sometimes God does not ask us to be successful, but just faithful.*
>
> *His hope was when he arrived in Abergavenny, that through strong biblical teaching and prayer, that at the end of his ministry the seemingly dead church would only want an evangelical pastor to succeed him. He imagined he might have ten years of ministry left as he was then 56 years old and said he would retire at 65 years, as he had seen too many people continuing to preach when their minds were past their best. In less than two years (in fact, twenty months), his vision and hopes were fulfilled. The church grew fast in his time there ... from just a handful of people to a full church and many people came to know the Lord.*[75]

Early on he was 'diagnosed with cancer ... and for that year he ministered out of a position of physical weakness'.

Ceri continues the story of her father's illness:

> *... he must have faced his terminal diagnosis with such courage as it couldn't have made a huge impact on our life at home. He*

---

75 Email correspondence, 28/01/2020.

continued as much as he could to pastor the church and preach and the congregation continued to grow ... in faith ... and prayer took on a new dimension.[76]

'It seemed a miracle', writes Mary Fielder, 'that the denomination had agreed to Jack being called to this congregation. One elder was a clear believer and understood the significance of Jack's ministry'[77] yet in late 1966 Jack Sharman was inducted as pastor of Whitefield Chapel.

One cannot but feel that he was God's man for the hour of need. Accustomed by a pioneering missionary background to attempting bold things for God, he stressed at the first church committee meeting that the church's actions must be positive and that it must go on the offensive with the gospel.

The challenge, however, was enormous. One Christian man from the small Baptist church nearby, engaged in itinerant lay preaching, had found preaching in Whitefield Chapel so hard prior to Sharman arriving that he decided not to preach there again. He felt it was 'dead' and 'hard'. What happened once Sharman began his ministry?

Response

Pegi Sharman thought she had met thirteen people in the town itself with a clear knowledge of Christ when they first arrived. Geraint Fielder reported that

When Mr Sharman came here, he found that there was no midweek meeting at all. When I came in 1969, I remember leading a group of nine people who had persevered in Bible study and prayer after Mr Sharman's death, having been encouraged to meet, first in homes and then weekly in church.

---

76 Email correspondence, 04/03/2020.
77 Email correspondence, 11/02/2020.

Ceri Douglass also refers to the church prayer meeting:

Another big change in the church was the midweek prayer meeting; this was a new thing and soon there was regularly a room full of people. One of the things that drew people to pray was when my father was diagnosed with bowel cancer, just a year after we arrived. Maybe this was the turning point of the church, and when Dad realised that his time there might be cut short, he prayed and preached with increased fervour.

Mary Jones takes up the story, relating her own experience. 'I read in the *Chronicle* that Mr Sharman was coming here.' Unhappy with her local village church because there was no Sunday School for her young boys,

I came one Sunday then Mr and Mrs Sharman visited me that same week ... I found him such a loving man, he made each person feel that they mattered and that he cared for them ... I was just a churchgoer ... but I knew they were different.

Mary was converted later under Geraint Fielder's ministry, but Mr Sharman

paved the way; he made you feel welcome and that's really important ... I think of Mr Sharman as being the person who opened the church up and let the town know that the church was here at this time.

Mary remembers other things about pastor Sharman:

I remember that when the fair came to the Fairfield, Mr and Mrs Sharman visited every caravan and the fair people said, 'We've never had someone visit us before' and they were really pleased to see them. They also went around the housing estates knocking on every door and making themselves known and we rapidly built up a very big Sunday School of children from non-churchgoing families on the housing estates. He did a lot in the short time that he was with us but I do remember thinking, and I still think ..., he was someone who seemed to me to have the gift of love and that was impressive.

Ceri Douglass confirms what Mary and others have shared:

Dad had an amazing pastoral heart and managed to get people to come across the threshold of the church and hear the message he was passionate about ... Dad also loved the farming community at the two branch churches at Fforest Coalpit and Pandy ... I also remember the week Dad was diagnosed with cancer, the fair came to Abergavenny, and Dad went to all the travellers and invited them to come to breakfast at the church ... I remember him also managing to persuade his dentist, Peter Davies, while having a tooth filled, to come with his young family to church, and both he and his wife Sue were soundly converted later.

Sue Davies relates what happened:

My late husband, Peter, arrived home one day after surgery and told me of an interesting gentleman who had asked him the question whilst sitting in the dental chair, 'Which church do you attend?' The gentleman was the new Presbyterian minister, Jack Sharman. So, the result of this meeting in the surgery, was that Peter said to me: 'We are going to Pen-y-Pound (Whitefield Church) this Sunday.' This was the start of our adventure with the Lord. Our son and daughter were duly whipped off on Sunday to the church's Sunday School by Mrs Sharman and came out smiling, imploring us to take them back the following Sunday. Pen-y-Pound became our spiritual home for many years.

Sue and Peter were converted later under Geraint Fielder's ministry.

A children's mission was held and evangelistic films shown at the town hall. Ceri Douglass remembers her father showing one of these Christian films for 'it attracted a big crowd and I can remember crowds queuing to get in and Dad asking for people who attended a church to leave and give their seats to people who didn't.' The church committee at the time expressed 'extreme satisfaction at and approbation of the venture'.

A youth leader was appointed and youth conferences commenced, with people coming to church in increasing numbers, especially to the morning service. Contributions more than doubled in less than twelve months. A new period of blessing had begun in the church and lives were being touched by the gospel. At a crucial point in this church expansion, a major setback threatened and by late May 1968 Jack Sharman had died. Ceri informs us that in hospital

> a few days before he died, he had a glimpse of heaven ... and wasn't sure whether he was in heaven or still on earth ... He shared with the Rev. Hugh Morgan, Newport, that he truly believed he knew what Paul meant when he wrote to the Philippian church 'For me to live is Christ, and to die is gain' (Philippians 1:21). This really impacted my life and, having known a father's unconditional love in my own life, I too wanted to follow the Lord Jesus he was so passionate about.

The church's W. K. Sharman Memorial Fund, supporting gospel work in Taiwan, is 'a reminder that the Lord takes to himself his servants but perpetuates his work in the heritage they bestow'.

Geraint Fielder

Having studied history in Swansea University, followed by theology in the Presbyterian College in Aberystwyth, and rather than enter into the Christian ministry immediately, Geraint Fielder succeeded Elwyn Davies as a staff worker with the Inter-Varsity Fellowship (now known as UCCF). He visited the Christian Unions in the Welsh colleges, advising and encouraging Christian students in their witness. At the end of a five-year period in this work, in June 1969 Geraint felt it was God's will to accept a call to pastor Whitefield Presbyterian Church. His ministry there spanned over ten years until 1981, when he became an itinerant preacher. At his induction service, Geraint recalls:

> *We had relied on Rev. Vernon Higham, the visiting preacher, bringing a stock of hymn books as we hadn't enough for a full church. He arrived with 100 books locked in his car boot. Unfortunately, he had forgotten the key. The service was delayed nearly 15 minutes while police tried to open the boot. It was eventually done with a spade! The hymn books were a gift from the church at Heath but seemed reluctant to join us!*[78]

Geraint continues:

> *In September 1970, the significance of our links with George Whitefield was reinforced. At the bicentenary of his death, commemorative services were held. The Rev. Dr Martyn Lloyd-Jones spoke to overflow congregations on Whitefield's life and work. What more appropriate challenge to us than the text of his evening sermon: 'Where is the Lord God of Elijah?' (2 Kings 2:14) ... and of Whitefield? ... and of all those other men who have been raised up at times of spiritual decline to call men back to repentance and faith? He is the living God still, and he alone can confirm and extend any work he may be pleased to begin. Where is the Lord God? If his Holy Spirit is powerfully within our hearts and his Eternal Son's lovely name is upon our lips we shall, surely, find that the Lord is here—in the midst of his church. And that is revival. So, what of the future?*

Progress

'When we arrived in Abergavenny,' Mary Fielder writes:

> *another elder and his wife had come to saving faith. Prayer meetings had been promoted by Jack and Pegi Sharman; they were always the*

---

78 'Do You Remember?' in the Church Magazine, *Contact*, early 1980.

128

barometer of spiritual health. There was a Sunday School, led by the very recently converted elder's wife

and also

a large lively youth club led by a believer … Some of these teenagers came to the Manse on Sunday evenings. We remember the first two girls to profess faith … Other groups developed as people responded to the gospel.

There was a trickle of conversions during this period and one key feature was that Christians were beginning to 'gossip' the gospel with unbelievers within and outside the church. Mary Jones, who had started attending the church under Sharman's ministry, recalls asking Geraint Fielder:

'How do you know when you're a Christian?' He said I should take John chapter 3, verse 16 and think about it. I remember I was helping out in the Sunday School at the time and I had a Billy Graham chorus book. I had gone home and I was playing through various choruses when John 3:16 suddenly seemed to be a light for me … and made me realise what being a Christian was—trusting in the Lord Jesus.

Susan Davies and her husband had been initially contacted by Jack Sharman and had started attending the church but

Geraint and Mary Fielder arrived a couple of years later, taking us under their wings, as they did with so many others. They were wonderful spiritual teachers; patient, loving and showing us so much grace—to two worldly souls. They were exciting times, as we heard the gospel preached so clearly, and suddenly the light shone into our lives, and we knew we would never be the same again.

Mary Fielder reminds us that

Geraint attended adult Sunday School in Gorseinon, taught by men converted in the 1904 revival. He never lost his roots. In

all his preaching he sought to connect and see a felt response. In preparation and post mortem appraisal he was never satisfied with simply declaring the truth, he wanted it to reach hearts.

Mary refers also to some entries in her diary: 'A measure of blessing again … tearfulness in many in the congregation'. Another entry reads '… every single person prayed home some aspect of the message. Pegi had a blessed time…' On another occasion, it was noted that 'Barry took communion for the first time.'[79]

But Geraint was not satisfied with a trickle of conversions because, encouraging as it was to see more coming to church, there were still the thousands who stayed away! Some attempts were made to reach out into the area with the gospel. In 1973 came the first National Christian Book Week and the Lord seemed to be telling us to take advantage of it locally. It proved a memorable venture … a large empty shop opposite Woolworths … was given to us free of charge for the week … twenty book parties were held in homes in the town. The entrance hall of King Henry School carried a large book display and one fifth-former, now a graduate, traces his conversion to the contact made while he was queuing for school dinner. The local bookseller estimated we'd sell about £20 of books. Sales topped £580. He was flabbergasted!

One result of this Book Week was a desire to hold

informal house meetings where the gospel could be discussed with friends and neighbours … so in September 1975 a team of 24 university students … spent 10 days with us … in holding house meetings … the gospel became a talking point, perhaps for the first time, in several homes … far more non-churchgoers attended these meetings than came to the two preaching rallies … many talked about

---

79 Email correspondence, 11/02/2020.

their need for Christ as they had never done before. Several people came into a greater assurance of salvation as a result of sharing their faith openly. Two dated their conversion from that week.

Christians, too, were greatly encouraged during these years. One example is Keith Williams, a university graduate working in the area who found Geraint's ministry to be 'rich' and 'fresh', so that he felt himself to be well-taught as a young Christian. The welcome and fellowship in the manse was valued, as well as the pastoral oversight. Keith states, 'It was an important period in my Christian life' as he, and many others, were grounded in the Word and taught how to read the Word. What may not have been appreciated by some was that the denomination was liberal in theology, so Geraint's denominational and interdenominational involvement 'was slender' as he used his energy on gospel activity; the message he preached was rare in the area. It was inevitable that 'after Geraint's ministry was established, believers in other local congregations, but starved of gospel teaching, came to join us. At one point we enjoyed believers from 13 different denominational backgrounds.' The church was also 'blessed by the arrival of believers to the area, who joined the church'. Mary Fielder continues, 'Employers such as ICI, those involved in building the Heads of the Valley Road, developing the local hospital in Nevill Hall into a District General Hospital, and industrial development all contributed' to the church's life and ministry.

Phil Hill

Having left Bristol Baptist College in June 1971, Philip Hill was inducted two months later into the pastorate of two Baptist churches near Abergavenny— Llanwenarth, Govilon, and Hope Baptist Church, Gilwern. The latter was small, with only twenty members, whereas the Llanwenarth church had about eighty members, but had no evangelical tradition. In fact, the previous pastor had been opposed to evangelical Christianity and accordingly Phil struggled settling into the church. The manse was not ready for about a month and he felt isolated having to stay in a local guest-house. Only about two young women in this church understood and appreciated his gospel preaching. But one significant means of blessing was his privately arranged meeting on Monday mornings for prayer with another pastor in the area. After they had met together for about three months, Phil refers to 'an amazing experience of God when we both felt compelled to fall on the floor humbled in the glorious presence of God.' In prayer, Phil was given a promise from the Lord that, despite the hardness of the people, he would see conversions under his ministry. Over the next twelve months, between thirty to forty people were converted, young and old, including families. Phil was also given a burden in prayer for the congregation and those to whom he witnessed. Opposition to his ministry continued, so after two years Phil resigned and entered into student ministry. Over thirty of the converts then joined Geraint Fielder's church in Abergavenny, with some going on to serve the Lord. This influx of new converts was a great encouragement for Geraint Fielder.

Prayer

Both under Jack Sharman and Geraint Fielder, prayer was encouraged in the church. Geraint wrote:

> When I was a lad, I remember our senior elder exhorting church members to attend the prayer meeting: 'The prayer meeting is the power house of the church; if that stops then the lights go out.'

Geraint then referred to the way Sharman re-started the church prayer meeting and that when he himself arrived only nine people attended, but slowly the number increased to about fifty. But he was not satisfied, for 'today, with more people of greater spiritual experience in the church, the numbers have halved, once or twice have fallen to only a dozen or so.' He posed the question:

> Why this decline when the Sunday congregations have continued strong? Whatever the causes, the decline must not be irreversible … Thankfully there are enough believers among us to ensure, God

willing, that the light will not go out again. But why leave the battle to the few? Things would change for the better this week: 'If my people who are called by my name humble themselves and pray and seek my face … I will pour out a blessing…' (2 Chronicles 7:14).

But what does this mean in practice? Geraint explains:

That means, if those who always intend to come but never get down to it, turned resolution into action; if those who come in fits and starts came consistently; if those who genuinely can only come occasionally actually come on the occasions they can come; if the elderly and the tired spent some time at home on a Wednesday evening joining with us before the throne of grace; if those who know they ought to come and have never done so asked the Lord if it might be they who are holding back the blessing with their disobedience…

Here, then, were strategic ministries which impacted the church and the town in Abergavenny and the surrounding villages.

Questions

1. What are your main impressions of Sharman's brief ministry in Abergavenny?
2. How did the church grow under Geraint Fielder's ministry?
3. '… humbled in the glorious presence of God …' Are there questions and observations you have concerning this experience and its significance for the church and pastor Phil Hill?

15. Looking Forward

This concluding chapter is reflective because we need to learn from the history recorded while acknowledging that we live and minister in the twenty-first century where the social, national and religious situation has changed radically. We cannot live in the past or ignore the contemporary challenges facing churches today, so reflection can be stimulating for us in our local situations. What follows in this chapter are bullet points identifying key aspects in the history recorded, then three Christian leaders provide their own reflections.

Pointers

- We glean from this history that churches do not survive on the basis of their past history. Sadly, few of the churches which experienced blessing in mid-twentieth century Wales are prospering today.
- There are numerous reasons why a church goes into decline and becomes a shadow of its past. These reasons, however, can be addressed prayerfully, often successfully.
- Congregations change in many ways, including the movement of members for a variety of reasons. Members grow old, stalwarts die, leaving a gap, while Christian teenagers after university usually obtain employment in other areas so home churches lose out, especially in rural areas.
- A church, if disengaged from its local community and remaining inward looking, will go into gradual decline.
- Without relevant, faithful preaching of God's Word and concern for the lost, coupled with quality pastoral care, a church will decline.
- COVID-19 restrictions have compelled churches to review their church life and local witness. Bridges need to be built with unbelievers and the community in very practical ways.

- The Lord is sovereign regarding when, how, where and for how long the Holy Spirit works more powerfully. Normally, unusual degrees of blessing continue for a short period rather than for years.
- A commitment to prayer by pastors and congregations for divine blessing on the preaching and teaching of the Word should be a priority.
- Rather than lament the lack of fruit in preaching, or criticise preachers, congregations need to focus prayer on the preaching of the Word. Only the Holy Spirit can make the preaching effective to unbelievers and believers alike.
- Christ-centred preaching, communicated well to a congregation and supported by fervent prayer in a context of love and mutual care, is a basic priority for a local church, despite discouragements.
- Are we open to the dimension of greater degrees of blessing and power upon the preaching of the gospel? God can break in unexpectedly, even in a small, struggling church.
- Reading of God's promises in the Bible and reminding ourselves of what the Lord did in Wales in the past can encourage us to pray and seek his intervention today.

James O. Fraser was evangelising the Lisu people of China early in the twentieth century, but most villages where he preached resisted the gospel for almost ten years. He appealed to Christians in Britain to pray, explaining:

> I am feeling more and more that it is … just the prayers of God's people that call down blessing upon the work … this increase can be brought down from heaven by believing prayer … We do our part, and then can only look to him, with others, for his blessing … Solid, lasting missionary work is done on our knees…

Eventually revival broke out amongst the Lisu, with many thousands of people being saved. The Lord is the same and can do this in Wales and in our local churches!

Rev Philip Swann (Llanelli Evangelical Church) writes:

This selection of accounts of blessing in Wales from the 1940s to the 1980s is unusual when seen next to the current experience of gospel churches in Wales. Few churches today experience anything of the dimension we read about here. There is a sense that these accounts could be discouraging as they show up the apparent spiritual poverty of our present situation. But, at the same time, they focus us on the heart of the matter for the church today—the glory of God seen in lives transformed through the message of the cross. They remind us of the necessity of the Holy Spirit's power to achieve this. At the same time, they encourage us to look joyfully and positively to the future of gospel work in Wales.

There are many cultural differences today when compared to the Wales of the 1940s to the 1980s. Whatever dying embers of chapel culture that were present during this period have long gone and we can no longer complain that people today are disconnected from church, as we now have generations that have never been connected with church. The secular culture that slowly brewed away around these accounts appears to have come to the boil today and threatens to boil over tomorrow. Our context today is very different, but the gospel we proclaim and the mandate we have to take it into the world has not changed. This brings us to the inevitable questions of how we impact the Wales of today and beyond with the good news of Jesus Christ?

It seems clear that this was the kind of question many were asking in the accounts we have here and they believed the answer was found in God. They did not pray to him out of a mystical or sentimental commitment to the idea of revival but rather prayed out of concern for the souls of their generation and community. It was the actual people and situations in front of them every day that gave them a heart and concern for their work, and they understood that evangelistic success depended on the work of the Holy Spirit. So, they prayed and worked, and prayed some more.

At the same time there is a general context for these accounts that is different to ours. The dying embers of chapel culture were present in their day and this was the context they worked with: liberal theology, two world wars and rapid social change were clearly generating indifference to the gospel, but there was still a connection with the idea of church among many people in their day. The apostles' approach to mission was generally manifested through evangelism in the synagogue, where the religiously sympathetic people, though strangers to the gospel, were found. Most of the accounts detailed are of God working powerfully in such a context.

As we look to the future and the mission of the church in Wales today, we see the context is different. In keeping with the apostles' approach, we see our context today is the market place, where people are disconnected from both the life of a local church and the message of the gospel. There is little in the way of the synagogue in Wales—no natural connection with church, no shared awareness of the value of Christianity, the Bible, or even God, in our communities. Church is considered irrelevant and increasingly seen as toxic in the minds of many. Worse still, Wales now sees itself as post Christian—a nation that has done Christianity and moved on, where the only remains are the hymns we sing at the rugby and the sight of our decaying chapel buildings. As we suffered in our COVID-19 pandemic, we saw no call to prayer from the Welsh Assembly—and why should we? They merely reflect the disconnected nature of our generation from God. God, to Wales, seems past his sell-by date or, at best, only good for Christmas and funerals.

This challenges us and, outside of the re-framing of all that the New Testament offers, it will discourage us. But within this framework it will fill us with great hope and even excitement, as we see mission in Wales is closer to the New Testament than even in the days of the accounts related here. The apostles' context of mission to communities with no awareness of the glory of God, or the message of the gospel, is our context. Today is not a time for despair or longing for the days of the past. There must be no place among us for the luxury of self-indulgent longing for the good old days, or for hunkering down in the relative comfort of prayer meetings for revival when there is no active engagement in mission. This is not the way of the New Testament and, thankfully, the way these accounts have been relayed has spared us the misery of this. Instead, we have been reminded of the means God always uses in his work in the world—his people connecting with communities, explaining the Bible and praying for the active work of the Holy Spirit. This was how God worked through the early church in its pagan, unbelieving context and it is the way he will work through us today to bring Christ to our families, friends, colleagues and neighbours. This is how he always works.

So, the way forward in the light of all this must be to give ourselves thoughtfully and creatively to the work of connecting with our communities, without any fear of doing things differently from previous generations. We must be more ambitious for the cause of the gospel, rather than sticking with the cherished methodologies of the past. We must give ourselves to the work of explaining the Bible to our communities as clearly as we can, in the most accessible of ways. We have so many common grace resources at our disposal and we need to explore and use them creatively in the plain speech of our day. We need to think in fresh and new ways that fit with the biblical principles of mission about how we connect our communities to the message of the gospel. We need to work diligently and creatively at finding where the listening and talking places in our communities are, and if they are not there, we need to create them. We need to be present with the good news of the gospel of God wherever these places are, no matter how uncomfortable they may make us feel. We need patiently to build genuine friendships with people within our unbelieving communities. We need to learn to love, listen, learn and look for the obvious and gentle ways we can enter in with the gospel. We must watch out for one another in the church with love and make sure the lives we live are better when compared to the lives of our unbelieving friends. Our lives should raise questions about our behaviour, for the right reasons. We must put right our obvious hypocrisies and self-first, self-comfort mind-sets when we see unbelievers among us. We must make sure our churches are genuine and transparent communities of people that are more attractive and compelling than any of the other communities around us. Churches must be seen to work and be communities of honour, safety, generosity, care, compassion, healing and love—communities where anyone, no matter how messed up or twisted they are by the dehumanising ravages of sin, knows they will be welcomed and loved with the good news of Jesus. And we must pray—we really must pray. Not pray at the end of all this for God to rubber stamp our efforts, but pray all the time and through all of this, and then some more. Pray with the awareness that we depend on God, and with the anticipation that he can do so much more than we can ever ask or imagine. We must pray for the glory of God above all things. Pray for the cause of Christ. We must pray for the broken, the comfortable, the unaware, the indifferent and everyone else, that Christ would work in their hearts through the message of the gospel in the distinctive and unmistakable power of the Holy Spirit. And we must pray that God will give us grace and strength to stick faithfully at all this, whatever the future may hold.

Rev John-Edward Funnell (Noddfa Church, Abersychan) writes:

In the last seven years, Noddfa Church has been transformed from facing imminent closure, with only half a dozen elderly members, to a three-digit congregation with a thriving youth work and Sunday School. The church, situated in the eastern valley between Pontypool and Blaenavon, is in an area cluttered with derelict coal mines, foundries, iron works and other heavy industrial sites that cover this once prosperous area.

Today, the valley is challenged by families experiencing fourth generation unemployment. The local schools have more than double the average number of children receiving free school meals in Wales, with over 70% of secondary school children in single parent families. We are top in the United Kingdom for children in the care system. Our valley is typical of a post-industrial area, suffering with high rates of poverty, crime, disability, unemployment, teenage pregnancy, drug abuse, domestic violence and anti-social behaviour. A plentiful harvest!

The population of the valley is approximately 10,000 people, of which I am the only resident minister. The valley is littered with closed and derelict chapels that had a combined attendance of less than thirty people when I started in 2014. Some congregations were as low as three elderly women and have since closed. Humanly speaking, we had less than a decade before the gospel light was totally extinguished in our area. We cried out to God in our emptiness and he graciously answered.

It was prayer-fuelled gospel preaching that revived the remnant into action. Through various touch points with the community, Noddfa Church began to reposition itself as a place of love and safety, drawing people in from a variety of backgrounds. Outreach varied from one-to-one conversations to big events like 'Carols Under the Arch', that welcomes over a thousand visitors each year. In 2021 Noddfa, was open every day of the week, serving hundreds within our community through various ministries such as homework club, youth work, supporting teen mums, toddler groups, Foodshare, homeless outreach and garden projects, alongside Bible studies across several demographics, prayer meetings, choirs and crafts. Over sixty 'repenters' were baptised during that period. God is moving once more in Wales and I am nothing but a bystander; all the glory must go to him.

In many ways, these have been the hardest years of my life. Early mornings and late nights have put a strain on my family. We have dozens of visitors a week to the manse as we serve broken and bored people living in a benefit dependent culture. Every day is a drama as we assist people with addictions, support them in court and work alongside social services, local schools and the police to pacify the aggressive and love the unloved. I have received 'emergency calls' regarding missing dogs, car breakdowns and fallen fence panels. Members have provided lifts to hospitals, re-roofed garages, cooked meals, picked litter, dug snow and delivered thousands of food parcels. We have dealt with tragic deaths and suicide, child abuse and obscene vice. But we take every opportunity in love to build a bridge for Jesus. I am just covering the tip of the iceberg here and much of the horror that I have witnessed over the years could not be published. However, in this struggle and frustration, as people have come and gone, I have had the blessing to see God move in such a powerful way. I have seen lives changed before my eyes and entire families transformed. Believe me, God has not forgotten Wales—the gospel still has power, even in the most unlikely of circumstances! It still offends and it still saves! Hallelujah!

Church decline is not because of cultural change; this is a poor excuse. The reason why people have stopped coming to church is simply because 'the church' has stopped living out the gospel. As a result, it has lost its position in our communities as the place of refuge when sin becomes a reality. This is the challenge for all churches today across Wales. Trust in the gospel and live it out.

Ten lessons learned

Noddfa Church is my first pastorate and I have made many mistakes during this season of blessing that have provided the lessons below.

1. Crisis

Every crisis is an opportunity for the gospel, but not everything is a crisis.

2. Let people go

The transforming power of the gospel also brings social mobility. Addicts have become clean, the marginalised have found community, families have reunited and the unemployed given jobs. Many who were so graciously saved have departed to seek greater opportunities and job prospects elsewhere. This is hard to manage as a church, but we must let these people go—we are not here to build empires, but to serve God's kingdom. He is building his church. Noddfa is just a small part of a long journey for so many of our congregation.

3. 'Church hoppers'

When God is blessing a church, you will find that many 'church hoppers' will try and jump on the band wagon. They come, promising the world, then let you down when they have exhausted whatever it was that they came for. Do not take it personally.

4. You are a pointer, not a fixer

Jesus is the answer; encourage those who come to you to follow him. Do not try to fix them yourself.

5. Order

In a world of chaos and destitution, people need someone who can provide order and professionalism. Be consistent, be reliable.

6. Love your core

Pray, empower and love your core. If you have a new idea that divides the church, park it. If they are happy to go ahead, prepare them for failure and try again.

7. Preach Christ, not culture

Our job is not to build a culture from the pulpit, but to preach Christ. From Christ, the culture will then follow.

8. God's Word

God's Word is a double-edged sword. Treat this as a warning. Use it responsibly.

9. The call

Ministry is a calling that must be tested; it is not a job. It is all absorbing and incredibly draining. If you have any romantic ideals of ministry, do something else because either you or your church will crumble.

10. Stick around

Ministry requires longevity and consistency. By God's grace, he has sustained me and my family for this long and I have only just begun to be accepted by our community. You will never know the importance of the word 'our' in the Welsh valleys. It has taken years of door knocking, arguments, abuse, being spat on, school assemblies, hospital visits, vandalism, court appearances, police interviews, carol services, community meetings, charity collections and break-ins for the people to call me 'our' pastor John. This is a name I will cherish for life and I pray that one day all will call on my Saviour as 'our Jesus Christ'.

Steffan Job (Assistant General Secretary of the Evangelical Movement of Wales)[80]

The Welsh language means different things to different people. To many Christians outside Wales, it brings to mind the great revivals of the past with Methodist Fathers and great hymn writers and preachers. To a growing number of people in the more populated areas of Wales it is an opportunity, as they see their children benefiting from a bilingual education. To others it's a sign of a nation recapturing its identity with prominence given to the language through celebrities and sporting achievements. And then to others it's the language of their heart—how they live, think, suffer, and rejoice. But what about the work of the gospel in the lives of the more than half a million people who speak the language—what is God doing in these communities today?

Setting the scene

Christianity has been at the core of Welsh language and culture for centuries. Place names, hymn singing at national sporting events, prayers in public, church buildings, Christian assemblies at schools are all signs of God's work in the past. But in the last century there has been a dramatic decrease in the spiritual health of the Welsh speaking people. Liberalism has had its effect, and we are now seeing the collapse of formal religion. COVID has only quickened the process with many churches not reopening. Although every Welsh speaker has been touched by some form of Christianity, the gospel is quickly disappearing from the land. Sprinkled throughout these communities are gospel Christians. Some find themselves on their own,

---

80 The following first appeared in the *Evangelical Magazine* March–April, 2023, pp. 12–13.

others have the blessing of being with others in small groups in either an Anglican, denominational or non-denominational church.

Gospel Christians and churches

Although gospel situations have not seen the dramatic decrease seen in other areas of the church, there is no doubt that many struggle. We cannot hide that we are not seeing conversions on the scale that is needed to fuel real growth in the church. We thank the Lord for all that he is doing, recognising that every conversion is a miracle, and that every person who is called into gospel ministry is a wonderful gift. Some gospel churches are being planted, some are seeing small growth, others are holding their own, but many honest gospel churches are decreasing in size.

The reasons for this are varied. The fact that every Welsh speaker has been touched by a form of Christianity (often dead and moralistic) makes it difficult to share the real Christian gospel message. There is also no doubt that there is an element of judgement on us all as a nation as we have turned our backs on God. But above all it shows that only God can save—he is sovereign, and we can't manufacture his blessing.

Is there hope?

We have a God who is love and loves to save. The Bible, history and our experience testify to this:

God is at work, and we are seeing conversions. Over the past twenty years we have seen many children of Christians and some people from outside churches coming to faith. The gospel is still the power of God unto salvation. We continue to see men and women being called into Christian ministry and a gospel unity across secondary issues.

Welsh speaking communities are not immune to the pressures that others are facing. Illness, poverty, uncertainty, death, and the changing of the morals of society are having an effect, and we are seeing an obvious need. For the first mission in many years this summer I met people who had started to read their Bibles and pray in search for help. Some people are searching, and we pray that God would bring these people into contact with gospel Christians and that the devil will not snatch the seed of the gospel away.

We are seeing a growing number of Welsh speakers linking up with English speaking gospel churches. Ironically, there may be fewer cultural hang-ups allowing them to hear the gospel through a non-Welsh speaking church! Many English-speaking churches have been asking for Welsh resources (such as Ask, our bilingual evangelistic Christmas magazine). What a wonderful blessing to see God reaching out to our fellow Welsh speakers through non-Welsh speaking brothers and sisters. Wales is fast becoming a bilingual country, and God may well be using this to reach and save Welsh speakers.

Welsh speaking Christians are becoming aware that we are missionaries in our own country. As Welsh speaking Wales becomes less Christian, as churches become smaller, and as we struggle to find full-time ministers, we become uncomfortable, and we are thrown on God. This is not always a bad thing for it brings us back to the basics. We are here to share the gospel as we travel homeward. It brings a focus on evangelism and personal costly devotion to God.

Our main hope as always is through prayer and a dependence on God. God loves to break in and save in hopeless situations. Though completely undeserving, he has broken into our lives as gospel Christians and placed us in Wales. It is to God we must look for an answer to the spiritual state of Welsh speaking Wales.

In the words of Habakkuk, 'Though the fig tree does not bud, and there are no grapes on the vines, though the olive crop fails and the fields produce no food, though there are no sheep in the pen and no cattle in the stalls, yet I will rejoice in the Lord, I will be joyful in God my Saviour'.

Four things to pray for Welsh speakers:

- Pray that Welsh speaking churches would have confidence in the gospel—it is easy to lose confidence when there is a lack of conversions.
- Pray that Welsh speaking Christians and churches would form stronger and greater links with non-Christians in their communities.

Chapter 15

- Pray for non-Welsh speaking churches and their work with Welsh-speakers.
- Pray that God would forgive us and bless us once again, for the glory of his Son.

Appendix

The Biblical teaching on revival

There is a very real danger of looking at the revivals which have occurred down the centuries and drawing principles from them in order to ascertain what constitutes a revival. Such principles are often used to colour the teaching of the Bible. In fact, we must begin with God's Word and consider what the Lord has to say and examine every experience of history in the light of the Scriptures.

As we consider some of the main points on this important subject, please have your Bible ready to look up every reference.

The Hebrew word which is translated 'revive' in the Old Testament has the basic meaning of 'to live', 'to preserve alive', 'to quicken'. We find the word used when thirsty Samson drank the water God gave him and was refreshed—Judges 15:19. In 1 Kings 17:22 we read that when Elijah prayed over the widow's dead son 'the soul of the child came into him again and he revived':

When the word occurs in a spiritual sense in the Old Testament, we note the main uses:

1. The revival of God's work generally; for example, Habakkuk 3:2.
2. The revival of God's people as a group; for example, Psalm 85:6; Ezra 9:8–9.
3. The revival of individuals; for example, Isaiah 57:15; Psalm 119:25, 37, 40, 50, 107, 149.

The English New Testament does not use the word 'revive', but the words 'to live', 'to quicken', etc. are the key notes in the Gospels. Jesus said: 'I am come that they might have life, and that they might have it more abundantly' (John 10:10). The word 'quickened' or 'revived' is used of the individual believer who was once dead in sin but is now alive in Christ (Ephesians 2:1). He has been revived from the dead through the action of the Spirit in the new birth (John 3:6–7).

Romans 8 tells us that believers are 'preserved alive' or 'revived' by the Spirit. While we are here on earth the old nature is always seeking to gain the mastery and so we are exhorted to mortify the deeds of the flesh. We are to 'put to death' the deeds of the body through the aid of the Holy Spirit, and in so doing we are preserved alive (Romans 8:12–13).

There is also a future aspect to this individual revival—the revival of our bodies at the last day (Romans 8:11). The Spirit who raised Christ from the dead will raise our mortal bodies (Hosea 6:2).

Because revival is not a New Testament word there are those who claim it is wrong to teach revival and to pray for it. We have already seen that it is to be the believer's constant experience, but what about revival in the church?

Let us consider three points:

1. The fact that the word 'revival' is not used is no ground for dismissing it. The word 'Trinity' is not to be found in the Bible and yet nearly every book in Scripture bears witness to one God in Three Persons. As for revival, the New Testament is full of awakenings in the life of the Church as a body and among individuals. The Acts of the Apostles is from beginning to end the outpouring of the Spirit upon the Church in revival. It was not something which occurred once for all, either. The early Church knew a continual flow of power (Acts 2:1–4; 4:31; 8:17; 10:44).

2. The New Testament is one with the Old Testament in stressing the need for the Lord to revive his people. Indeed, it is the fulfilment of the prophet's message to a wayward and rebellious people that the Spirit of God came down at Pentecost in reviving power (Joel 2:28; cf. Acts 2:16). Although Pentecost was a unique work of God, it was also a reviving of God's work among his people.

3. In the book of Revelation two churches in particular are exhorted to consider their need for reviving grace. Sardis had a name for being alive,

but it was dead (Revelation 3:1). The summons is to 'be watchful' or a better translation is 'awake'. There was an 'awakening' or 'revival' wanted. Again, to the self-sufficient church of Laodicea our Lord reveals that they need to realise their poverty and nakedness and come to the only one who can truly refresh and restore them (Revelation 3:17–20).

As we survey the Old and New Testaments, we see the clear teaching to be:

1. Revivals are the supernatural action of God. Even the obedient response of God's people to fulfil the conditions essential to the promises of revival as laid down in 2 Chronicles 7:14 is by God's grace. Only the Lord can truly humble us, give us repentance and a praying spirit (cf. Psalm 119:32; Acts 5:31; 11:18).
2. All spiritual decline is through man's sin and results in God's judgement. The cry for revival is coupled with a realisation that God's wrath is upon all disobedience (cf. Psalms 80; 85; Habakkuk 3:2; Revelation 3:3,19).

In revival, the Lord, who is the fountain of life, is seen acting in grace, giving life to those who walk in darkness and preserving alive a people to the praise of his own glory. Such times of refreshing will cause the Church to experience great power in preaching, great grace and great fear in the fellowship (Acts 4:33; 5:11).

Rev. Philip H. Eveson
(Church Magazine April 1972,
Malpas Road Evangelical Church, Newport)